HEY, U UP?

(FOR A SERIOUS RELATIONSHIP)

HOW TO TURN YOUR BOOTY CALL INTO YOUR EMERGENCY CONTACT

HEY, U UP?

(FOR A SERIOUS RELATIONSHIP)

HOW TO TURN YOUR BOOTY CALL INTO YOUR EMERGENCY CONTACT

EMILY AXFORD + BRIAN MURPHY

ABRAMS IMAGE, NEW YORK

Editor: David Cashion
Designer: Devin Grosz
Production Manager: Alex Cameron
Illustrator: John Devolle

Library of Congress Control Number: 2017949415

ISBN: 978-1-4197-2914-0
eISBN: 978-1-68335-236-5

Printed and bound in the United States
10 9 8 7 6 5 4 3 2 1

Abrams Image books are available at special discounts when purchased in
quantity for premiums and promotions as well as fundraising or educational
use. Special editions can also be created to specification. For details, contact
specialsales@abramsbooks.com or the address below.

ABRAMS The Art of Books
195 Broadway, New York, NY 10007
abramsbooks.com

We dedicate this book to you, cutie ;-)

CONTENTS

IV. *LONG-TERM RELATIONSHIP* ————————————————— 103

V. *MOVING IN TOGETHER* ————————————————— 123

INTRODUCTION

When you're single, it feels like you're surrounded by happy couples. You imagine all of your friends in relationships constantly having mind-blowing sex, occasionally coming up for air and candlelit steak dinners. In your head, all they do is bone and brunch and go on hikes and ignore your text messages. Somehow, they've managed to thrive in the very same dating pool in which you are currently drowning. What's it going to take for some hot lifeguard to finally pull you out? And maybe let you live in their penthouse, rent-free, because they also happen to be rich? You know, one of those wealthy lifeguards, who works by choice.

Why does it seem like everyone can find love but you?

You are, objectively, a great catch. You are a learned person who reads books (apparently), you have enough disposable income to buy books (presumably), and you have a great sense of humor because you're enjoying this book so far (definitely). *You* should be the one having tantric sex in your king-size bed with your conventionally attractive soulmate and ignoring *your* friends' texts about the weird bird they just saw.

But your friends' relationships aren't as glamorous as they seem. For every romantic getaway that they document on Instagram, there are twenty-six Costco runs, eighteen mandatory family gatherings, and at least two fights about whether or not they should get insurance on the rental car. In fact, they're jealous of you! *You* don't have to attend your nephew-in-law's christening this weekend! You're free to waste your whole Sunday on a hangover. Single people have no one to hold them accountable!

Everyone wants the companionship and security of a relationship, but with the passion and enthusiastic oral sex of being single. It's like that movie *Blade*, where Wesley Snipes has the advantages of being a vampire without any of the weaknesses. Is that too much to ask? To get all of the good parts of a relationship, without any of the bad? And to have vampire strength, but also be immune to wooden stakes?

Well, we're here to tell you that you *can* have it all. Because we found it.

We are Murph and Emily. Before we got together, we knew each other as coworkers at CollegeHumor.com. That all changed when we got a little too tipsy at a work party and ended the night dancing naked to Frank Ocean. It was sweet. It was romantic. It was the most 2012 thing you could do outside of voting for Mitt Romney.

Our secret office romance was secret for about two hours, and we continued to raise eyebrows when we moved in together after only three months. The general reaction was a mixture of concern and awe. As our friend David put it, "This is either going to end in marriage or murder-suicide." Luckily for us, it ended in marriage!

We got engaged six months in and married shortly thereafter at a wedding venue that a cultured person might describe as "reminiscent of a medieval hamlet," but we described as "mad *Lord of the Rings*-y." Since getting hitched, we've continued to work together as comedy partners, collaborating on a ton of successful (and unsuccessful!) Internet, TV, and, now, literary projects. If you don't know us from *Hot Date*, College-Humor, or *Adam Ruins Everything*, you would probably recognize us as that couple in your Facebook feed that occasionally pops up having sex in a comedy sketch. We haven't made the shift to actual porn yet, but who knows what will happen if this book doesn't sell!

Somehow, we manage to work together, live together, and sleep together without killing each other. We've got what everybody wants and what every so-called "qualified" relationship expert says isn't out there: *Someone Just Like You That You Also Want to Bone*. It's for this reason that our friends, skeptical at first, now come to us for advice: "How can I be like you? How can I find my soulmate and nail them down, in no time flat, after a series of rash decisions?"

We'll show you—out of the goodness of our hearts, but also to fulfill our publishing contract. This book is a step-by-step guide through every stage of a relationship. We'll take you from your first hookup to consummating the marriage doggy-style. If you're already in a relationship, there is still plenty to glean here, but you could always skip ahead to the section that best applies to you for Maximum Glean™. If you're single and/or know how books work, just start at page 19.

Be aware: some of our advice is not to be taken literally. This is comedy, after all. Ahead are a series of satirical stories and essays that can be applied to your own life as you see fit. You know, like the Bible. Also, like the Bible, we recommend you start pushing this book on all of your friends and maybe even go door-to-door asking people if they're ready to accept Murph and Emily into their hearts. If any hotel managers are reading this, feel free to place this in every dresser in your establishment.

We promise it has almost as much weird sex stuff as any holy text.

HOOKING UP

–Our Story–

We got drunk at a work event
and went down on each other.

I.

This book is about finding your soulmate. And the first step to finding your soulmate is to drunkenly make out with your soulmate in the back of a cab that you'll forget you paid for until you look at your bank statement. Welcome to the hookup scene! We hope you brought a travel toothbrush.

Navigating this hive of scum and villainy (and, in some cases, HPV) can be tricky. How can you be sure you're hooking up with The One and not some jamoke who just happened to look good in the low lights of that painfully self-aware dive bar? You can't. You can, however, up your chances of knockin' boots with The One if you narrow your pool of potential hookups. Maximize your chances of going home with a winner by ruling out the losers. You'll thank us when you don't wake up on an air mattress next to a thirty-four-year-old wannabe DJ named Klaus.

STOP HOOKING *DOWN* AND START HOOKING *UP*!

Let's be honest. You don't always make the best decisions for yourself. Sometimes you miss the FedEx delivery because you're too scared to answer a phone call from an unknown number. Sometimes you go to the McDonald's and order the Quarter Pounder Value Meal instead of the much more sensible Fruit 'n Yogurt Parfait. Sometimes you stay up all night just so that you can "sleep" on your three-hour flight to Houston the next day. Then you're too tired to enjoy Houston's famed Lyndon B. Johnson Space Center!

You do the same thing when you sleep with someone who should be below your standards. Like somebody who doesn't have a job, or even worse, somebody who works in social media. That's not hooking *up*. That's hooking *down*. And you're not going to sleep your way to The One by hooking down.

Let's examine some of the people you're likely to run into on a night out. Bring this book to a bar and we'll help you sort the creepers from the keepers. Go ahead, we'll wait. We'll have two of whatever you're drinking. Two for each of us.

...

COME ON! A TGI Friday's? You don't want to have sex with someone who's been eating loaded potato skins all night. Let's go somewhere that doesn't have snowshoes on the wall.

...

OK, that's better. Now look around. Who do you see?

- *A guy with a Macklemore haircut.* Why shouldn't you pounce on this trend-hopping fashionisto who may or may not know his haircut is identical to the signature 'do of the Hitler Youth? Because he might be a Nazi. Or, equally distressing, he brought a picture of Macklemore to his barber and said, "Like this." Either way, this guy is a serious **HOOK DOWN!**

- *A girl with purple hair.* A girl with purple hair is like a horse wearing a fake horn. The first time it was done, everyone was like, "Wow, cool! A unicorn! How unique and quirky!" But then a bunch of horses started doing it and it stopped being special and you stopped believing in unicorns. As interesting as it might seem at first, having sex with a horse is a major **HOOK DOWN!**

- *Some dude with a leather messenger bag.* Nothing says "I'm ready to be a live-in boyfriend" like a leather messenger bag. Because inside every leather messenger bag is a leather-bound moleskin notebook. And you know what's in that? *Feelings*. This is a man who thinks and feels, and feels and thinks, and would love nothing more than to feed you his signature pancakes and teach you how to make French press coffee after you **HOOK UP** on his tasteful leather couch. So much leather!

- *A woman with bangs.* Bangs take *maintenance*. Which means she's responsible. Not to mention, there's a 95 percent probability that anyone with bangs likes baking.[1] Which is perfect, because you like eating. Enjoy the smell of fresh red velvet cronuts while you **HOOK UP**. (NOTE: If those bangs are uneven and freshly cut, STAY AWAY.

---

1   After all, bangs are the apron of the face.

This recently dumped hot mess hasn't even started the *Eat* phase of her post-breakup *Eat, Pray, Love.*)

- ***A grown man in a novelty T-shirt.*** Some people say puns are the lowest form of wit. We disagree. Wearing a T-shirt with a pun on it is the lowest form of wit. The only stretch bigger than the forced wordplay is the literal stretch of his medium T-shirt across his soft, doughy chest. If you've got to pull off a shirt that says "Fruit Lupus" with a picture of Dr. House eating Froot Loops, then you're **HOOK-ING DOWN**. This also applies to novelty hoodies that double as costumes. If your date can turn into a Stormtrooper by zipping up his sweatshirt, he is exempt from blowjobs.

- ***A lady drinkin' a whiskey.*** What is it about whiskey that attracts the most *adult* people? Not only will her kisses taste like a wood chipper in Vermont, but she's clearly classy as shit. Luckily for you, classiness can be sexually transmitted. So **HOOK UP**.

- ***The DJ.*** Avert ye eyes and heed not the siren's call! Or rather, the siren's electro-haus mixtape. We guarantee that when you get back to his place, you're gonna be sleeping on a mattress on the floor of an air conditioner–less room. Avoid this **HOOK DOWN**, unless you want to receive Facebook invites to his "sets" for the rest of your life.

- ***Someone who's there with their dog.*** A doggy drinking buddy? Borderline irresponsible, but undeniably ADORABLE. **HOOK UP** with this animal lover and receive a free dog for the duration of your relationship! You'll never have to pay vet bills or walk it when it's raining! And if you feed it treats behind its owner's back, it will like you better.

- ***A minor celebrity that you kind of recognize from something.*** Whoa, is that the guy from *Suits* on USA? Or maybe he's the dude from *White Collar*. Definitely one of those shows with suits in it. Either way, your parents definitely watch the show and they'll be super impressed if you bring him to Thanksgiving. Fucking a basic cable superstar? Now that's **HOOKING UP!**

Unfortunately, bar hookups have a low success rate. Since most people's buttholes clench the moment a stranger speaks to them, we recommend you don't waste your time approaching total randos. They'll label you a creep before you even get to do any of the creepy stuff!

Instead, invest your time in *kind of* randos—that sweet spot between stranger and acquaintance. A kind of rando is someone you've never met before, but have a tenuous connection to: a friend of a friend, someone in your adult dodgeball league, the paramedic who revived you after you were knocked out cold in your adult dodgeball league.

When you share a common interest, you can bypass the social vetting that a total stranger would endure and get straight to layin' pipe and fallin' in love. And, if things don't work out between you two, there will be little to no social consequence. They're just some *kind of* rando, after all!

EXAMPLES OF KIND OF RANDOS YOU SHOULD ZERO IN ON

- *Your roommate's friend who's in town for the weekend.* Anyone from out of town is usually down to do something stupid, like hook up with you. If things go well, they've got a built-in excuse to visit again. If they don't, who cares? They live in another city! Simply *don't* take a three-hour bus to Boston and you'll never have to see them again.

- *Other people at this weirdly horny convention you're at.* Whether it's a business conference or AnimeCon, if you're gathering at an event space in a hotel, you've got a good chance of getting laid. Maybe it's because you'll be attending meet and greets with drink specials in a bar three floors below your bed. There's no fifteen to twenty minute taxi ride to second-guess your "chemistry" with Caitlin from the Ohio branch. Action - thought = sex!

- *Someone wearing the same sports jersey as you.* Rooting for the same team makes you allies. And what do allies do? They high-five. That's constant, excited, physical contact. A few *up highs*, a couple *down lows*, maybe a *too slow* to show that you've got a sense of humor, and you're in. If your team wins, what better way to celebrate than by scoring your own home run? If your team loses, what better place to drown your sorrows than someone else's butt cheeks?

- *The barista who works at your local coffeeshop.* Attractive, cool, mysterious, and attentive to your every need—is this your fantasy come to life? Or are they just a person working in customer service? Sorry, playboy, it's definitely the latter. As a general rule, don't read into any interaction that involves a tip jar (or a tip G-string).

- *Someone from class.* Avoid anyone you see on a weekly basis in a room with unflattering fluorescent lighting. This could be continuing education classes, learning a new language, improv, etc. Especially improv. Watching people try to be funny is stressful enough. You don't need the added anxiety of finding out that someone you dirtied the sheets with still does the Borat voice.

- *Someone who has the same morning commute as you.* Whether it be by train, bus, car, or, heaven forbid, elevator, you do not want to have to see your ex every day. Hooking up with the toll booth lady might seem like a great idea now, but do you really want to reopen your emotional wounds every time you hand her a quarter and feel her sweet caress?

- *A coworker.* Obviously, it's on a case by case basis. We were coworkers and it was smooth sailing for us! They say not to shit where you eat, but it turns out it's actually OK if you have a casual work environment where everyone is cool eating in a big office full of shit.

Once you've set your sights on that hot piece of pseudo-stranger ass, it's time to go in for the *chill*. Engage them in a private conversation that discourages anyone else from joining. Questions like, "What was growing up in Ohio like?" and "How many kids went to your high school?" are only interesting to two people: the person answering them, and the person trying to sleep with the person answering them.

MANIPULATE SOMEONE INTO SLEEPING WITH YOU BY BEING GENUINELY INTERESTED IN THEM

Successfully nailing down your hook up requires DECEPTIVE PICK UP TECHNIQUES like "listening" and "making a human connection." If you want this person *eating out of the palm of your hand*, try this MASTER CON: ask them a series of personal questions, based on a genuine curiosity about who they are as a person.

People like to talk about themselves. EXPLOIT THIS WEAKNESS by BAITING THEM into engaging conversation. POUNCE on the opportunity to relate to them on a deeper level. THEIR VULNERABILITY is one you share—two souls, wandering this crazy planet, just trying to make sense of it all.

When you're SCAMMING your soulmate into enjoying your company, TAP INTO THEIR DEEPEST DESIRES. One way to do that is to ask them, "What are your deepest desires?" Then, when they answer, listen. If you want to totally PULL THE WOOL OVER THEIR EYES, you can even ask thoughtful follow up questions. This kind of PSYCHO-LOGICAL MINDFUCKERY shows that you are interested in what they are saying.

Here are a few topics of conversation that will BAMBOOZLE this SUCKER into feeling like a living, breathing, human being who matters:

- *their favorite hobbies*
- *what their childhood was like and how it shaped them*
- *where their career is now and where they'd like it to be*
- *their favorite vacation they've ever been on*
- *what their major was in college*
- *their relationship with their parents and how it shaped them*
- *their favorite movie, television show, or book*
- *if they believe in God or the idea of a soul that is metaphysically separately from the body*

Once you've laid your TRAP, all you have to do is wait for your PREY to GET CAUGHT and accept your invitation to speak candidly about the things that matter to them. If they say something that you relate to, TURN THE TABLES by offering personal information about yourself, painting a picture of *your* values and what has shaped *you*. There is nothing like a rewarding, reciprocal conversation to COMPLETELY HOODWINK someone into wanting to spend more time with you. Regarding someone as an equal is the best way to GET IN THEIR PANTS.

If you guys are drinking, this is going to be easy. No one is more comfortable speaking about themselves in excruciatingly personal detail than two drunk people who want to smoosh sexy parts. By the time you hear yourself say, "It's not that my dad wasn't *physically* around, as much as he wasn't *emotionally* around," you're well on your way to sealing the deal. They may even want to do it right then and there, in the bar bathroom! Being classy goes a long way, so remember to use the stall.

However, if you or your red-hot rando don't want to *get down* immediately, let your phones do the fuckin'. When you can't swap spit, swap numbers.

HOW TO INFECT THEIR PHONE WITH THE VIRUS OF YOU

In this day and age, asking for someone's phone number is down-right *rapey* (short for *rapacious*, meaning overly aggressive or greedy). That's why it's always a better strategy, upon meeting someone you'd like to have telephonic access to, to just give them *your* phone number.

Offering your number makes them feel safe, but it also gives the impression that you are a cool, casual person that lets life happen to you. You are as chill as they come. You are like a Taoist, meditating upon a lotus petal, allowing the whims of the wind to style your hair! Little do they know, you use enough mousse to give a full-grown male lion the Macklemore (again, for any lionesses reading this, remember that Macklemore lions are a hook *down*).

So how do you give them your number in a way that guarantees they'll call? First off, you need their phone. Since reaching for some-one's phone is almost as intimate as reaching for their genitals, make sure you ask permission first. A casual "Can I give you my number?" followed by something *hilariously playful* like "I'm not trying to read your texts," should do just fine. In the unlikely event that they insist on putting it in themselves, there are a few pressure points in the wrist that will cause them to release the muscles in their fingers.

Now that you've acquired their phone, you can really make a lasting impression. Inputting your contact info is *crucial* to the flirting process, because you can give yourself a cute name like "Jeff Bar Hottie" or "Liz Gorgeoussupermodelsexyandsurprisinglysmart." Don't just write "Jeff" or "Liz" or you'll blend in with all the other Jeffs and Lizzes and the next time you hear from this person will be as part of some mean party game where they have to call someone in their phone who they don't know. Don't be the dunce who gets put on speaker phone at a party you weren't invited to.

Once you've entered your contact info, don't stop there. Follow yourself on all social media apps and enable push notifications. Pretty soon you'll be popping up all over their phone, so make a mental note to post old photos from your skinny phase and pics from vacation that make you look rich. When they open their feed the next morning and see a picture of you in Costa Rica, twenty pounds lighter, they'll think "Wow! This person is so much hotter and better traveled than I remember! Also, how did they make it to their flight on time? I was just talking to them four hours ago."

Finally, the masterstroke: Before you hand the phone back, text yourself so you have *their* number! Boo-yah, bitch! You just had your cake and ate it too. You got to look like a chill non-creep, but still ended up with their number *and* an active text thread. Their phone is now infected by the Virus of You. You're a handful of flirtatious texts away from getting *skintimate*.

Depending on the audience, your text flirting could be an innocent exchange of winky-face emojis and *It's Always Sunny in Philadelphia* gifs. Other times, the conversation will descend into utter depravity. So make it the kind of depravity you can be proud of.

After your disgustingly adorable meet-cute, you'll likely make plans to "hang or whatever next weekend or something." But that means at least five to seven days before you see each other again—an eternity in horny person years. How do you stay fresh in their minds?

Send nudes.

Sexting can be stressful. If they don't respond to your *hawt* pic instantly, you'll convince yourself you've been uploaded to a revenge porn site with your apartment geo-tagged. The inherent risk of sending nudes out into the airwaves is that someone other than the desired recipient might see it. Whether a mutual friend catches a glimpse of your nipples after scrolling too far in your fuck buddy's phone gallery, or your dick pic is passed around a bar booth of giggling women, the threat of exposure is real. The only solution is to make the pictures so hot that you *want* everyone to see them.

The key is to emphasize your assets without looking like you're emphasizing your assets. Yes, your dick looks big when you take a close-up shot at a low angle and your cleavage looks good in a high-angle selfie—but those tricks haven't fooled anyone since our grandparents were sending their tits via telegram. If you're going to pull a *fat* one on them, you'll have to be more creative. With a little ingenuity and the right props, you can make a baby carrot look like a fully matured root vegetable. Or a pair of tangerines look like a couple of genetically modified grapefruits. Mmmm, pulpy.

Quarter for Scale Illusion

① Tape a quarter to a wall.

② Position your erection several feet in front of it.

③ Pretend to be holding the quarter, which looks like a dime next to your "huge" dick.

It's a Banana in My Pants and I Am Happy to See You

① Place a banana in your briefs.

② Stretch your penis along the length of the banana.

③ Poke the head of your actual penis out of the bottom of your briefs, creating the illusion that your stretched-out penis has the girth of a large tree fruit.

Touched by Dolls

① Place a doll's hand on your penis.

② Frame it so it looks like the doll's hand is your hand, which is dwarfed by your penis.

③ Send the pic, then a follow up with a shot of your real hand to prove that you don't have baby hands.

Wet T-shirt Cluck-Test

① Insert two huge chicken cutlets under a white tank top.

② Center two Hershey's Kisses to look like nipples.

③ Drench the shirt in water and win the wet n' wild contest of his heart.

Doggy Style

① Cover a dog bone in makeup so that it matches your skin tone. You know, one of those dog bones that looks like a wand with a big butt at each end.
② Use a hair tie to make a tiny thong for one of its butt-shaped ends.
③ Hold it close enough to the camera so that it is indistinguishable from a real butt. It now appears that you have a plump butt and tight midsection like an ideal woman/dog toy.

Fun-Size Bikini Top

① Write "Hot Bitch" on a child-size bikini top.
② Squeeze yourself into said bikini top.
③ Take a picture of what looks like your huge boobs in what couldn't possibly be a child's bathing suit because it has profanity on it.

──────── FOR THE LADIES AND THE FELLAS ────────

Cocktail Winner

① Place a cocktail wiener between your breasts or next to your erect penis.
② Send along with a message that says "Wanna come over? I'm making foot-long hot dogs ;)"
③ Pretend to be horrified when the picture leaks: *"Oh no! Now everyone knows I have a perfect body!"*

After that steamy text exchange, we can only assume they showed up at your doorstep and did you right there in the foyer. Noice! Collect your high five on the next page!

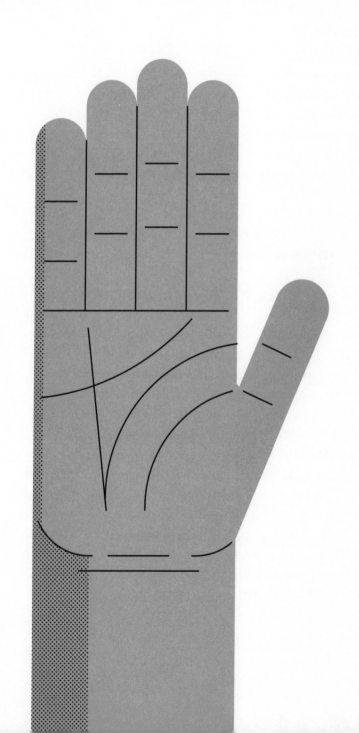

How was it? For guys, hookups basically rank from Jizzed a Little to Jizzed a Lot, so we're not worried about you. For women, it can be a little more complicated. That's why we're going to take a break from our gender-neutral relationship guidance to speak directly to you. Ladies, if you're not having mind-blowing sex right out of the gate, have a little patience. Key word being "little."

ARE YOU SEXUALLY COMPATIBLE?
(KEEPING IN MIND HE GETS FIVE TRIES TO GIVE YOU AN ORGASM)

So, you hooked up with a new guy and you *really* like him. He's sweet, funny, has a good job, and you're already daydreaming about getting on his health insurance. Great! Except, one problem: you didn't O. It was a Fourth of July without fireworks. A roller coaster without the *big* drop. You climbed all the way to the top of Mount Everest and there was a sign that said PEAK CLOSED FOR RENOVATION. The O from earlier stands for orgasm, did you get that?

If Prince Charming hasn't found your glass slipper yet, don't fret. That's **totally** normal. Don't give up on him just because he didn't rock your toe-socks the first time! That's ridiculous. It might not click until the third, fourth, or even fifth hookup! That's why you should give him *exactly five tries* to bring you to orgasm.

Look. Rome wasn't stimulated to ecstasy in a day. You can't expect a new guy to crack the code to your climax vault the *first time*. You shouldn't expect that until the *fifth* time. So stop worrying! Until the fourth time. Then you can start worrying.

Guys are easy to please. Women? Well, think about it this way: Each woman is like a different musical instrument. Sure, it helps if he has *musical experience* (and rhythm!) but each *instrument* requires a different technique. Just because he's played the trombone doesn't mean he's going to be an amazing sax player right away. You'd need to play the saxophone at least five times before you completely mastered it.

Men place *a lot* of pressure on themselves to perform. If he's feeling down, be reassuring: "Don't worry, you get four more tries!" "Three more tries!" "Just two more!" "This is it. Make it count." Let him know that the bedroom is a judgment-free zone! Until the fifth time he sets foot in it.

There's another factor that may be lurking, or should we say, *slouching*: he might experience *erectile difficulty*. Again, this is fine. He could be drunk. Or in his head! Maybe he jerked off three times today because he didn't want to prematurely ejaculate, but now he's got nothing left. An otherwise good guy deserves the benefit of the doubt. The benefit of the doubt being four free passes followed by one last Hail Mary to prove his masculinity.

Truthfully, it would be a good idea for him to get a handle on his erectile issues early. Ideally he figures it out by the second or third time so he still has a couple attempts left to decipher the mystery of your orgasm. We'd like to say we offer some kind of golf handicap to these guys, but sadly, no.

In the end, though, true love is worth the wait. If you're patient, you will be rewarded. Unless you're too patient, in which case, you're just wasting your time with some chump who can't deliver the goods. Yes, love is *kind*, but it'd also be *kind* of nice to cum. And he already had five tries.

Annnnnnnnnnnnnnd welcome back, gentlemen! Our gender-blind exploration of the dating world will resume now. And what is something that all genders, sexual orientations, and species can enjoy?

69-ING YOUR WAY TO A MORE SATISFIED YOU

Oral sex is the first car on the train to orgasm station.[2] But what if your partner tries to jump ahead to sex? Or what if they opt for some unenthusiastic hand play? What if, Eros the Sex God forbid, you go down on them and they don't return the favor? You'll have to rethink your positional strategy and create conditions that are favorable to reciprocation. Refer to the figures below.

This is your end goal. A side-by-side 69.

---

2   Yes, anal sex is the caboose.

Yes, it requires that you also give oral sex. You cannot expect to be on the receiving end of hawt action if you are not willing to dole out hawt action. This is the kind of generous behavior that all strong relationships and super-hawt 69s are founded on. But how do you get yourself to this position? The key is in the transition.

Let's start with a standard makeout.

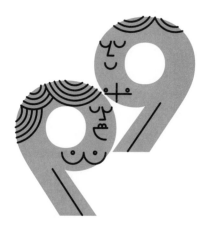

Then you, a selfless saint, start going down on them . . .

**. . . but flip around so you conveniently leave
your junk within spitting distance of their face!**

Your partner has all the tools to succeed right up in their face. Remember, this is only a *suggestion*. You're merely making it easy for them to make the choice themselves. It would be rude to smush a Big Mac in someone's face, but it's perfectly fine to give them a ride to the drive-thru. If they just happen to order a Big Mac because, hey, it's right there, great! We're lovin' it.

You might be asking, "Why can't I just go down on my partner the normal way without angling my genitals at them?" You can, but you run the risk of doing something nice for someone without getting anything in return. Like in the case of dudes who watch too much porn and think unreciprocated oral sex is normal.

Not only does the side-by-side 69 beat out other methods of oral sex, it also boasts a subtlety lost on the other 69s, which are likely to backfire—crawling on top of your partner requires you to sit on their face (rude!) and swinging them upside down for a standing 69 is as uncomfortable as it is a freakishly intimidating feat of strength.

As a general rule, you shouldn't do anything in the bedroom that the Undertaker might do inside a steel cage at WrestleMania. That is, unless you're the Undertaker's wife, in which case, this fun role reversal is likely to titillate. For everyone else, side by side is a perfect way to come together.

...

By now, you should be an elite level hookup ninja, ready to be dispatched by sexy feudal lords. But getting your sheets dirty with a different whatstheirface each week will never be enough. You want more. Flowers. Romance. Someone with a cooler apartment that you could just, like, move into.

So how do you know when you're on the right track? The fortune teller has her crystal ball, but you've got something better: a hot plate of eggs and a Bloody Mary.

PREDICT THE FUTURE OF THE RELATIONSHIP BY OVERANALYZING BRUNCH

Brunch is like a relationship job interview. Last night's hookup was merely an email with a résumé attached. If they want to be considered for the position, they need to slay the next step of the process: a conversation in broad daylight over huevos rancheros.

Between the hangover, the lack of sleep, and the postcoital jollies, brunch is a particularly vulnerable time when you can learn a lot about your potential mate. Invite them out for mimosas. If they say yes, they might be interested in more than just a fling! The question is: Are you? Don't think of this as a meal, but rather a series of tiny tests with which you will make sweeping judgments about them as a person. *Observe*.

- **What did they order?** Meal choice says a lot about a person. *Steak and eggs?* Aggressive. Expensive taste. Three months into the relationship you'll discover they maxed out their credit cards on a protein shake pyramid scheme. *Fruit and granola?* Meek. Cheap. You'll spend your Sundays going on hikes and brewing homemade deodorant. *Pancakes?* It isn't even noon and this jamoke has reached their carb quota for the week. Do you really want to be with some slob who thinks taking naps is a hobby? *Eggs Benedict?* A blue-collar protein with a hoity-toity sauce—this person's a goddamn wild card.

- **Did they get a drink?** On the surface, a Bloody Mary is the masculine brunch choice, while a mimosa is more feminine (only excess testosterone could fuel a decision as bad as ordering ketchup vodka over delicious, boozy OJ). But we must dig deeper. Did they order a drink because they're a free spirit who wants to keep the party going? Or because they're an alcoholic who is trying to delay the shakes? If they didn't order a drink, it's possible they don't drink at all. That's perfectly acceptable if it's in a cool "I partied too hard and have a bunch of stories" way, but be on the lookout for the *never-had-a-sip* types. You don't want to be around someone whose unflinching self-control shines a light on your shithead lifestyle!

- **How hungover are they?** Ideally you're both groggy, but in a way that is visually appealing. Messy hair, but like you spent a day at the beach. Eye makeup smeared, but like a glamorous smoky eye. Head-ache, but in a playful "don't talk to me until I've had my coffee" way. Anything more and you may be dealing with a lightweight. If you date someone who can't hang, you'll be spending your weekend mornings scooping puke out of the sink and spoon-feeding them Gatorade.

- **Who paid?** If they offer to pay, great, so long as it's not some ostentatious display of wealth or heteronormative values. While they're signing the check, try to sneak a peek at what kind of gratuity they're laying down. You don't want some trust-fund bruncher who can't properly tip on their four Pink Lady mimosas, but you also don't want some psycho who writes a "hey sweetie" note to the waitress.

  If they let you pay, great, so long as they pretend to reach for their wallet. Only a career freeloader wouldn't make such an easy and ultimately empty gesture of respect, and relationships live or die by empty gestures of respect. Like offering to carry the lighter of their two bags at the airport or yelling, "You OK?" when you hear them stub their toe in the other room.

  Ideally the two of you will split the check, which is a lot like 69-ing because you both give a little while you're eating out. And you know we're all about that.

Of course, you can always opt to stay in and make breakfast. That's what *we* did after our first hookup. This is a great choice if you are hoping to turn your one-night stand into a one-night-then-again-the-next-morning stand, or if you're trying to hide your scandalous intra-office tryst from prying public eyes. Or in our case, both!

If you don't know how to cook, don't worry. When it comes to taste, you can always replace "good cooking" with "bad for you." You burned the eggs? Just sprinkle Doritos on them and call it a South of the Border Scramble. Your pancakes have the consistency of a sinus infection sneeze? Pour that failure over ice cream and call it a Sunday Morning Sundae. You overcooked the hollandaise sauce? That's your fault for trying to make hollandaise sauce with a hangover. Just use ketchup next time, you pretentious fucking foodie.

If you're looking for the perfect post-hookup recovery meal/pre-hook-up fuel, check out the next page for the actual recipe we made the morning after our first hookup. We promised our readers a recipe for a great relationship, but who knew we'd be so literal! Hopefully you won't get diarrhea like we did. If your stud or studette passed the brunch test, it's time for you to get *battle*-tested. Onto the emotional warfare that is dating!

BUFFALO CHICKEN OMELETS

INGREDIENTS

- 6 eggs (get the most expensive ones, most expensive = most-ethical murder farms)
- One of those rotisserie chickens you always see at supermarkets
- Pre-crumbled blue cheese (spend the extra $$ to avoid the hassle of "crumbling")
- Hot sauce

PREPARATION

1. Butter your skillet. Crack the eggs onto the skillet. Realize, a little too late, that you were supposed to whisk the eggs then feverishly try to whisk them in the pan as they cook.

2. Peel off pieces of the supermarket rotisserie chicken while trying not to wonder how long they let supermarket rotisserie chickens sit under the heat lamp. Add those pieces to your scrambled "omelet." Add blue cheese liberally.

3. Pour hot sauce until one of you says "stop." Since you are both trying to impress each other, that's gonna be a while: "Oh yeah, I looooove spicy food. I'm just a cool risk-taker like that. I love danger. Medium wings don't make me cry."

4. Serve in Tupperware because you haven't done dishes in a while.

DATING

-Our Story-

We had sex and sometimes
went to restaurants.

II.

After you've been *hanging out* (see: boning) for a bit, you may decide that you like this person enough to *date* them. Nice! Dating is pretty much the same thing as hooking up except that you are occasionally seen in public together. Double nice! Oh, except, add feelings. Whup!

Dating is the awkward space between *Hooking Up* and *Being in a Relationship*. You take the bad parts of hooking up (sexual insecurity) then add the bad parts of a relationship (emotional vulnerability) for a meaty, toxic stew. You're like a cartoon character, straddling a gap between two shifting tectonic plates: precarious, unstable, and totally spread-eagled.

The period when you're *Dating* but not *In a Relationship* is not a straight line as much as it is a maze of confusing detours, sexual tangents, and amorphous relations between two or more people. It's an unnecessarily complicated world, filled with vague rules that are constantly being redefined and questions that never get answered. Basically, it's like *Lost*. So how do you know if you want to start something that might, in the end, leave you disappointed and unfulfilled? Easy!

So long as you have a graphing calculator.

SHOULD YOU DATE? AN EQUATION

Since you can't trust your mushy little heart to decide what's best for you, let's turn to cold, hard *algebra*.

$$\{(x * [y/5]) + ([a+b\text{\textasciicircum}2]\}\text{\textasciicircum}3\pi/z = ?$$

x = how good the sex is on a scale of 1–10

y = how good the conversation is on a scale of
   1–"who cares, the sex is a 10"

a = # of mutual friends

b = # of mutual *couple* friends

z = proximity of their apartment to yours, in minutes

CONFUSED? WE'LL WALK YOU THROUGH IT.

Let's say that *Jane* is hooking up with *Joe*. Jane and Joe are having g-spot-shattering sex (10), but seem to have nothing to talk about once it's over. Jane is also beginning to suspect that Joe is an idiot, based on the fact that he's "never heard of" Portugal (1). They also have no mutual friends, other than McKenzie Lytle, who they both hate (0). That'd be a death knell, *except* that Joe lives literally two blocks away. Wow! Joe went from a 2 to a 26!

Or maybe *Leo* is bumping uglies with *Chandra*. It's going great (10) and during their postcoital chat sessions, Leo and Chandra discover they share a love of hiking and cooking classes (9). Gross, but better that they date each other and stay the hell away from the rest of us. Leo met Chandra through some friends from high school who went to college with Chandra (5). The problem? Chandra lives fifteen subway stops and a forty-five-minute commuter train away. Yikes, Chandra could have been a 23, but that commute kicked her down to a 1.61104151. Something tells us that Leo is going back to Rachel—his kinda busted, super-mean ex-girlfriend who lives in his building.

Finally, take *Jarvis*, who is doing the deed with *Tucker*. Jarvis says Tucker takes it like a dead fish, and Tucker is slightly disgusted by Jarvis's coital wheezing (0). Making conversation is like trying to pin a thumb tack to a brick wall (0). However, Jarvis and Tucker are literally the last two people left in their close-knit friend group (14) entirely of couples (7). Factor in a ten-minute drive between their apartments and round up: Jarvis and Tucker are looking at a 50! A convenient, albeit miserable, relationship awaits them!

...

Go ahead. Reduce your hookup-buddy to a series of numbers, and see if they're worth dating. If you get a 5 or more, you have our blessing to ask them out on an official date. Sure, it seems backwards to ask someone out *after* sleeping with them, but this is the sexy world we live in!

HOW TO ASK SOMEONE OUT ON A DATE AFTER YOU'VE ALREADY SLEPT WITH THEM

Like any good millennial coupling, you've gotten to know each other biblically before getting to know each other the regular way.

You've been face-to-face with their genitals, yet you still don't know what their favorite band is or if they have any siblings. How do you penetrate the one orifice you haven't explored: *their soul?*

Since you've already had this person's pubic hair stuck in your teeth, asking them to meet you in a crowded bar at 6 P.M. should be easy, right? Wrong! When you ask someone on a date, you're putting yourself out there. But in, like, a different way than you did when you let them lick your butthole. Going on a date requires you to use your tongue in a whole new way—to talk about things. Deep things. Personal things. Things like what sports you played as a kid or what you think of the food you are eating.

So how do you summon the audacity to ask someone you've already doinked on a date? If you're feeling nervous, try the age-old public speaking technique: picture them naked! This should be easy considering you have already seen them naked, on multiple occasions, from a variety of angles. If it helps, you can take it a step further and picture yourself naked as well, then recall vivid memories of the two of you banging. It should ease your fear of rejection a bit to remember that you've already spanked them.

Study this person's body language to see if there's a mutual interest. Be sure it's their nonsexual body language, though. A gesture in the sheets is very different from a gesture in the streets.[3] *Do you ever catch this person looking at you?* Like, when you're hanging out, not when they are going down on you and imitating what they've seen in porn. *When they touch your arm, do they let their hand linger?* Again,

---

3   Imagine waving at someone in bed. They would be very confused!

during nonsexual hangouts. If you are mid-bone and they do that, they probably mean "faster" or "harder" or "will you eat spaghetti off my butt, it's always been a fantasy for me." *Does their face light up when you enter?* The room, of course.

If any of these physical cues sounds familiar, this person might be into you! Or maybe they just wanna sleep with you again. Who knows, really? This is the bed we millennials have made for ourselves and now we have to lie in it. Too bad we didn't make a restaurant, so we could sit in it. Like on a date!

When you do finally summon the courage, make it clear that you're asking them out on a real, genuine date. This is not some casual hang followed by a night of sloppy sex. This is a restaurant hang followed by a night of sloppy sex. Those two things are different for some reason. If they decline, don't be discouraged. Just because they have tasted your secret juice, doesn't mean they're ready to be seen in public with you. They might just want to keep it casual and hang out in a no-strings-attached, only-a-piece-of-rubber-stands-between-us-combining-our-DNA-and-creating-a-life-together kinda way.

If they say yes, however, you are in for an adventure. Many exciting and terrifying things await you. How will you navigate these treacherous lands of Dating? Luckily, ancient Elven cartographers have already mapped it out for you.

THE TREACHEROUS LANDS OF DATING: A MAP

THE CASUAL HUMPS

THE ILLUSORY PEDESTAL

THE I WANT SOMETHING MOORS

THE FORTRESS OF A RELATIONSHIP

THE INSECURITREE

THE RUINS OF OLDE RELATIONSHIPS

THE WHAT ARE WEEDS

MOUNT OGAMOUS

STILL SEA-ING OTHER PEOPLE

① THE ROLLING HILLS OF CASUAL HUMPS ━━━━━━━━

Here, simple folk who don't want drama live a no-labels lifestyle void of responsibility, commitment, or catching feelings. Though you may tarry here awhile, someday you will heed the call of adventure and explore a life beyond being someone's backup booty text.

② THE ILLUSORY PEDESTAL ━━━━━━━━

As you wander through idyllic pastures with your new companion, steer clear of the Illusory Pedestal, for all who are put on it will appear impossibly brilliant and hot. Be warned: dark magic is afoot! No man or woman can live up to the image you have created for them. The only way off the pedestal is down. And they can't stay up there forever! There's no bathroom.

③ THE I WANT SOMETHING MOORS ━━━━━━━━

The path narrows as you enter the I Want Something Moors. Arriving at this ominous realization, the air chills and clouds gather. Here grows the ancient InsecuriTree, whose roots reach far beyond the lands of Dating. Step with care, traveler. Dark caves of defense mechanisms and unexpected geysers of emotion lie ahead.

④ THE WHAT ARE WEEDS ━━━━━━━━

The foggy uncertainty of the Moors gives way to a labyrinth of over-growth. Hindered by thick vines and the protruding roots of the Insecuri-Tree, you must navigate a tangled mess of feelings without scaring anyone off. There is also a troll named Ol'gar who will grant you a wish if you can beat him at Xix (that's troll chess).

⑤ MOUNT OGAMOUS

Should you make it through the awkward foliage of the What Are Weeds, you'll emerge at Mount Ogamous. From these exclusive peaks, you can see the unshakable Fortress of a Relationship beckoning on the horizon.

⑥ STILL SEA-ING OTHER PEOPLE

A wrong turn at the What Are Weeds, however, and you may end up Still Sea-ing Other People. In these choppy waters, you must sail past the Commitment-Phobic Fjords, the Maelstrom of Mind Games, and the ever-enticing Island of Better-Looking People.

⑦ THE RUINS OF OLDE RELATIONSHIPS

There's no way around it. Before you enter the Fortress of a Relationship, you must pass through the Ruins of Olde Relationships. The specter of their last relationship, and, honestly, everyone they've ever hooked up with, will haunt you here. Also, if you did defeat Ol'gar at troll chess, he will be here to challenge you for "double or nothing wishes." He is a very sore loser.

⑧ THE FORTRESS OF A RELATIONSHIP

Should you survive the dark lure of relationships past, you have proven yourselves worthy. Lay down your bindle and rest, weary traveler. You're finally safe within the secure walls of a relationship. Go forth, and fart freely.

Of course, there are many paths from the Casual Humps to the Fortress of a Relationship—so many twists and turns that it can't all be contained in one map (magical as the elves who created it are). The only way through is to be true to yourself.

And if that doesn't work for you, try being someone else!

WHO TO PRETEND TO BE, OTHER THAN YOUR GARBAGE SELF

Dating and *deceiving* share more than just a first and last consonant. The beginning of any relationship is marked by two things: a lot of sex, and pretending to be someone you're not. You dress nicer, shower more frequently, and suddenly, you're super opinionated about music. Why? Because for some reason, personality = your favorite bands. We blame *Garden State*.

When creating your new, non-garbage identity, think about the person you are seeing as the main character in a movie. Then cast *yourself* as the romantic interest. Who should this manic-pixie-dreamboat be? Remember, they shouldn't be anyone who exists in real life—"recently divorced dad who's just started dating again, but mainly out of obligation" doesn't exactly give off a Ryan Gosling vibe. And we can assure you Margot Robbie isn't embodying male fantasy as "girl whose job has her traveling a lot right now, so she's kind of stressed out, and also she recently started to wonder if she should freeze her eggs."

Since it's difficult concocting an entirely new identity from scratch, we've come up with a casting breakdown of unrealistic characters that you can play for 1–3 months. You'll be their greatest fantasy come to life! At least until you feel comfortable enough to reveal your garbage self.

Cool Girl Who Likes Whiskey and Sports

FEMALE, EARLY 20s. Cool Girl Who Likes Whiskey and Sports is an enigma. A *girl* who likes *whiskey? And* sports? B-b-b-but, those are *guy* things! Cool Girl Who Likes Whiskey and Sports has a DGAF attitude and can beat you at *Halo.* Her nightstand is a pile of graphic novels and *Simpsons* figurines. She says things like "I just get along better with guys," and "I don't have that many girl friends." You don't even think to question what a pathetic thing that is to say because holy shit, she's wearing a *Futurama* shirt (total dude show!!!!). She hates everything girly, likes everything dudes like, and does it all authentically. That's just who she is. It has nothing to do with courting male attention. She holds her liquor like a frat boy, scarfs late-night pizza like a stoner, but still has the body of a nineteen-year-old pilates instructor.

Super Comfortable in His Masculinity Guy

MALE, MID 20s TO MID 30s. Super Comfortable in His Masculinity Guy is vulnerable and open. He is unafraid to show his emotions, even though he grew up in a society that shamed them. Sometimes, when he is expressing himself, he does it with a perfectly weathered acoustic guitar. He isn't afraid to wear the latest fashion and keeps a dream journal, which he has to take his man bracelets off to write in. If you asked to read his journal, he would be fine with it, because he is not cagey at all. He has none of the bad masculine traits like being aggressive, competitive, or objectifying women but has all of the good ones, like being strong, building furniture, effortlessly growing a beard, and having a nice dick with those little pelvis lines that look really good on guys. He has no issues with his dad and a bachelor's in women's studies from Sarah Lawrence. Oh, but he calls it a *bach-*

elorette's, because "why is the default always masculine?" He's not weird about having sex during your period. Dating him is like being in a lesbian relationship with a lumberjack.

Smart Girl Who Doesn't Know How Beautiful She Is

FEMALE, EARLY 20s. Everyone loves a Smart Girl Who Doesn't Know How Beautiful She Is. She is one of the most beloved tropes in film, television, graphic novels, and One Direction songs. Even though we live in an age where we can take unlimited pictures, post them on infinite websites, and get immediate feedback on our appearance, she, somehow, still has no idea that she is a 10 across the board. If you asked her what she looked like, she'd probably shrug and say, "I think I have brown hair?" How would she know? She's too busy studying and reading. Oh, but not in an intimidating way. She doesn't use all her smarts to dominate a traditionally male career or make more money than you. She uses them to start a nonprofit or open a muffin shop. That way, you can admire her drive and ambition, but still see how she'd be willing to give it up and raise your children. All of your friends have crushes on her, but if you told her, she would deny it, then change the subject to children orphaned by the Syrian crisis. Also, even though she doesn't think about it, like at all, her body is just naturally banging.

Guy Who Likes Your Girlfriends

MALE, MID 20s TO MID 30s. The Guy Who Likes Your Girlfriends is down to go out dancing or stay in and watch *Empire* with a bottle of wine and your friend Tara, who just got dumped. When he meets your friends, not only does he not silently sulk or exclusively talk to their boyfriends, he asks them questions. Like they are real people who still matter even though he can't sleep with them! Groups of four or more women don't scare him. Oh, but don't worry, it's not like he has his own girlfriends for you to be intimidated by. His best friend is you and his circle of friends is your circle of friends. Except when you want to go out for a girls' night. He's totally cool with letting you do your own thing.

Party Girl Who Is Still Low Maintenance

FEMALE, EARLY 20s. Party Girl Who Is Still Low Maintenance wants to party-all-the-time-party-all-the-time-party-all-the-tiiiime, but never has any of the bad side effects that are associated with binge drinking and taking mountains of drugs. She loves to go out boozing, but never slips up and gets too drunk or needs to be taken care of. If she does ecstasy on Saturday, she's still perky and fun on Sunday morning. She knows a lot of people who own boats, and spends most weekends partying on them, so if you hang out with her, you do too. She's carefree and doesn't need to label her relationships, so she's down to keep things casual as long as you want. She knows how to dance to dubstep, and when you are with her, so do you. She always has drugs on her, but has never once asked you for any money for all the drugs she's shared with you. Despite all this, she still has a stable, well-paying, full-time job. Also, her body is banging.

Person with a Secret, Tortured Past

MALE OR FEMALE, ANY AGE, UNLESS FEMALE, IN WHICH CASE EARLY 20s. The Person with a Secret, Tortured Past is interesting and mysterious. Unlike most people who have endured trauma, however, they are still emotionally available in every other way. They ride a motorcycle and have tattoos that are super meaningful and super personal. They are basically a jigsaw puzzle that you get to slowly, patiently put together. A very attractive one. Even though they have a painful, secret past, they are not afraid of love. On the contrary, they want you to help them heal, so they are very open with you. But also brooding. Like if James Dean was really good about texting back.

...

As you can see, most of these characters are self-contradictory and/or don't exist. Yet, here you are! Your date will feel like they've stumbled on the Holy Grail, when really, you're just a regular ol' cup pretending to be the Holy Grail! After a couple weeks, you'll probably even fool yourself into thinking you aren't garbage. And hey, Kurt Vonnegut says we are what we pretend to be, so in a way, you aren't even lying!

Now that we've aided and abetted your total deceit of this person, it's important to be sure that they aren't deceiving you.

FIND OUT IF THEY'RE PLAYING MIND GAMES WITH YOU
BY PLAYING MIND GAMES WITH THEM
. . . WITH A *SELECT YOUR OWN "VENTURE"*![4]

While you are working overtime to trick your partner into thinking that you're cool, they may be doing the same. What a turnoff! Why can't they just be themselves? Or at least a carefully constructed movie archetype like you?

---

4 Title changed for trademark purposes.

The only way to find out if they're playing you is by playing them. Dating is about finding companionship, but it is also about winning. Begin with Section 1 and follow the instructions until you get *YOU WIN* or *THEY LOSE*.

1

You reactivate your Tinder account and find the profile of your current squeeze. When were they last active? If it was today, *go to section 2*. If it was a week ago, *go to section 3*. If it was before you were dating, *go to section 4*. If you want to search the secret catacombs beyond the garden, *go to section 9*.

2

Your brow furrows. Why would they need to be active on Tinder when they're dating a cool and attractive person such as yourself? Something's fishy here. Better dig deeper. You create a fake Instagram of a hot but attainable stranger, then send out follow requests to their whole social circle. Once you've built up a believable number of mutual friends so they won't suspect that you're a bot, send a message claiming to have met them at a party and ask them out for drinks. If they say they can't because they're already dating someone, *go to section 4*. If they agree to go out for drinks, *go to section 5*.

3

You've been dating for a few weeks, but they've only stopped using Tinder this week. Is that because they started to fall for you this week? Or are they just taking a week off to focus on all the booty calls they've built up? If you've been hanging out a lot and it's unlikely they have a secret cache of side pieces, *go to section 4*. If they've been inconsistent, but only because they're "super busy," *go to section 8*. If they've been straight up bailing on you, *go to section 2*.

4

This is good. *Too* good. It's time to test them. When you hang out next, go to the bathroom and leave your phone out with Tinder open, giving them the impression that you are still actively looking for other people (in the middle of your hang, no less). When you get home, check to see if they've logged onto Tinder as revenge. If they have, *go to section 2*. If they haven't, *go to section 10*.

5

This is bad. They're surfing Tinder, meeting strangers for drinks, and dumb enough to be catfished by you. You have no choice but to show up to the trap-date and confront them about their total breach of trust. After you pop out and scream at them in the middle of a crowded bar, how do they react? If they tell you to fuck off forever, *go to section 6*. If they beg for your forgiveness, *go to section 7*.

6

This total maniac was making plans, dates even, with other people and *they* think *you're* the crazy one for deceiving them with an elaborate trap? *THEY LOSE!* Kick 'em to the curb before they kick you!

7

You have the upper hand. They now know that you are smarter than them *and* they feel like they owe you something. *YOU WIN!*

8

Ooooo! Mysterious! We hate mystery. Continue dating this person for a week, but keep your guard up. If they drop the Criss Angel act and tell you what they've been "super busy" doing, *go back to section 1* and try again. If they get more mysterious, *go to section 12* to confront them about their behavior.

9

You travel through the garden into the catacombs and notice an old bookshelf covered in spiderwebs. Amid the collection, you find a dusty old tome. As you pull it out to investigate, you hear the sounds of complex machinery clanking. Suddenly, the entire bookcase moves to the side. A door! Behind it lies a narrow labyrinth with a torch lighting the entry. To follow the path, *go to section 11*. To ignore this weird side track and get back to reading about relationships, *return to section 1*.

10

Congratulations, you are dating a total peach. A gem. A peach with a gem in it instead of a pit. *YOU WIN!*

11

You pull a torch from the wall and suddenly the bookshelf closes behind you. You are trapped. With no other choice, you wander the halls of the labyrinth until you happen upon a hooded figure. Suddenly, your phone vibrates and you're reminded that you've gotten really off track. You check the phone to see when your crush was last active on Tinder. If it was today, *go to section 2*, if it was a week ago, *go to section 3*, if it was before you were dating, *go to section 4*, if you want to confront the hooded figure, *go to section 12*.

This sketchy person reveals themself to be a goblin and murders you. *THEY LOSE!* You also lose, though.

Anyone who survives the insane booby-traps that you've set is a keeper! Or a brilliant mastermind who has beaten you at your own game, in which case, they're still a keeper. Those sociopathic skills will lead to a great career in business and you can ride their coattails!

Either way, once you've realized what a catch this person is, you might find yourself wondering: "What's going on here? We hang out, we have fun, I'm really starting to like them . . . *what . . . are . . . we . . . ?*"

Whoops! You did it. The second those words enter your brain, it's over. You've entered the spider-filled labyrinth of the What Are Weeds and there's no turning back. The words can't be unthought. It's like how a bag of chips is never-ending until the second you think, "Wow this bag of chips is, like, never-ending" and it promptly ends.

In the absence of an honest conversation, you can always . . .

DEFINE THE RELATIONSHIP BY OVERANALYZING HOW THEY INTRODUCE YOU TO THEIR FRIENDS

If you want to know how this person feels about you, pay attention to how they introduce you to their friends. In that split second, they will be forced to make a spontaneous decision that you can project a million insecurities onto. Are you a valued partner or a living, breathing sex toy? It's important to really overthink it. Stay up all night if you have to. There is no limit to the mental CPU you can commit to this task. Feel free to reallocate RAM that you set aside for other things, like eating and remembering to call you mom.

"This is my boyfriend / my girlfriend."
The relationship is defined! Unless they used sarcastic air quotes. Or were those just excited jazz hands? Remember, you can overanalyze body language too!

". . . the girl / guy I'm seeing."
OK. That's something. The answer to "what are we?" is you're *seeing each other*. But what does that mean exactly? Everyone has a different idea of what seeing someone means. For some, it means dating exclusively. For others, it means they're seeing you, in addition to a bunch of other people (aka they're on a fuck tour and now you have to get an STD test). Unless they meant they're seeing *you*, specifically, when they picture their future husband/wife . . . Yeah, that's probably it!

". . . the girl / guy I told you about."
Nice! Except, what exactly were they telling their friends about you? Because you've told your friends about a lot of people, for a lot of different reasons. You told them about that amazing date you went on with that mixologist who was getting their PhD in paleontology, but you also told them about the person that threw up on you in the middle of oral sex. So, like, which end of the spectrum do you fall into here? Probably PhD, right? You've only barfed on their junk like twice, and that's hardly enough to get a reputation for it.

"... the girl / guy I told you about from the party."

If you're the girl/guy from the party, that would suggest that there are other girls/guys from *other* locales. Probably a girl/guy from the café, all cute and tatted up. At least one girl/guy from the bar, also all cute and tatted up. Some girl/guy from work, who probably has tattoos but has to keep them covered up because of office policy. Wow, you're gonna need to get some tattoos if this is going to work out. Unless you already have them, in which case, you're totally their type!

"This is [your name]."

OK, not much meat on these bones. On the surface, it seems like a good sign. Their friends know your name! They don't need any context to describe who you are! Unless they've never heard your name until this moment, and your partner only said it because they've literally never mentioned you. But that just means they've never talked shit about you! This is good, really good.

"This is ... I'm sorry, what's your name again?"

This is admittedly, not good. Definitely ripe soil for tilling insecurity. Not all is lost though. Maybe they aren't used to a foreign, exotic name like yours—Jessica. Just remind them! Maybe show them your driver's license. Some people learn better visually. Blame the pollen in the air when your eyes start to tear up as you shake their friends' hands.

"This is [someone else's name]."

Lots to unpack here. Once again, lemons that you're going to have to, through sheer mental gymnastics, turn into lemon tarts. If you're really good at self-delusion, you could probably convince yourself that the other name they called you is a code name they use when they journal about how they're falling in love with you on their secret blog. You know, even just writing that, we started to believe it! Who doesn't have a coded blog these days?

"... the chick/dude I'm banging."
Wow, brag much? Someone's proud of you! ... Is what you'll tell yourself while you shake hands with a group of people that, after that introduction, do not respect you.

"... that pathetic nobody I text when I'm horny."
This one seems pretty damning. We think it's safe to say the two of you are not on the same page. There's a silver lining, however: they've definitely mentioned you to their friends!

"[Nothing. They don't introduce you]."
Not much to analyze here. Unless you want to try to analyze their body language as they stare past you like a stranger. But what does "cold, unfriendly eyes and the faint sneer of superiority" *really* tell you about how they're feeling? Ooo, we know, maybe they're intimidated by you!

...

Once you've met their friends, you can begin to put together a picture of their life and how you fit into it. But in order to complete this masterpiece, you'll need to look to the past. Fortunately, the past has a public Instagram.

At some point, they'll mention their last relationship in passing. Something like, "Oh, I did that with my ex, [INSERT DUMB NAME OF DUMB EX]." You'll laugh it off, get quiet, and count down the minutes until you're alone so you can go full Anonymous on this jerk.

Browsing an ex's feed can make you feel a little insecure. But that's ridiculous! You should feel *very* insecure. Here's a breakdown of potential posts you might encounter, and why they make you, by comparison, inferior:

- *A picture of their new tattoo.* Wow. Their ex is so artistic. Based on the "newest addition!" caption, it's safe to say this isn't their first one. Imagine how exciting it must have been to continually uncover new tattoos, like Easter eggs, hidden all over their body. This is a person who doesn't overthink things. Unlike you, who's been talking about getting the state you grew up in inked on your ankle for seven years but still hasn't even Yelped a tattoo parlor.

- *A picture of a sign that says, "Nashville, 38 miles."* Oh no, this person is a total free spirit. Wandering this way and that. A slave only to the summer's gale. You can't compete with that! This picture's probably from some spontaneous road trip they spontaneously went on, using only whimsy as their GPS. Imagine all the impromptu *"let's rent a car and just drive"* weekends they must have shared. The last time you rented a Zipcar, you visited Grandma.

- **A picture of an iced coffee next to a David Foster Wallace novel.** Dear God. The nights the two of them must have spent, naked and wrapped in purple satin sheets, debating DFW's use of metaphor as a vehicle for sarcasm. Their insights sparking the imagination. Their musings shedding new light on the previously misunderstood. Every day with them was probably like getting a PhD in *life*.

- **A picture at a protest.** Uh oh. This spontaneous free spirit who reads big-kid books is politically active in the way that YOU SHOULD BE. While you were tweeting supportive hashtags, they were in the streets, boots on the ground, changing the world. How are you supposed to fill those activist boots? They probably say stuff like "rebellion" and *don't* immediately think of *Star Wars*.

- **A screenshot of an FKA Twigs song.** Crap crap crap. This freaking dreamboat *gets* music you don't get. They listen to experimental pop and think, "Wow, this is good" not "Shit, is this what I'm sup-posed to like now?" They probably go to live concerts and don't even leave early to beat traffic. The fact that you've seen Mumford & Sons three times isn't gonna cut it with the recent memory of this goddamn indie pop savant haunting every moment. Time to go down a Pitchfork rabbit hole and try to learn the difference between tUnE-yArDs and Dirty Projectors.

- **A vegan smoothie.** No. No. No! That perfect skin you were hoping was just the result of really good lighting is actually the product of years of acai bowls, tofu scrambles, seitan skewers, and ethical dining. Think of all the healthy shits this person takes from not eating a plate of nachos they made with Doritos instead of regular tortilla chips because, "What the hey, it's Sunday!"

- **A gym pic.** What? What??? Is there a God?[5] How can a veritable genius of literature and music *also* have the faint lines of a six-pack? How do they find time, between poetry readings, cliff jumping, and doing ecstasy at M83 festivals, to cultivate that kind of muscular tone? You can't compete with someone whose mind and body transcend the limitations that plague the rest of us mere mortals. Time to go punish yourself with push-ups. Then drown your sorrows in a big plate of Dorachos.

- **A photograph with THE PERSON YOU ARE DATING AKA YOUR SUPPOSED-TO-BE-FUTURE-BOYFRIEND/GIRLFRIEND IN IT!!!** Oh shit. This is bad. *Real* bad. You scrolled all the way back to when they were a "we." Nothing left to do now but panic and read way too deeply into their beaming faces. Honestly, their micro-expressions read like novels. Really happy novels. So . . . nothing like novels. In fact, the longer you stare, the more their casual euphoria looks like a smug sneer, gazing out of the phone at you, judging you for scrolling through Instagram while taking a shit without a shirt on. Only one way to calm these nerves: create a dummy account, follow the ex on all platforms, then *Single White Female / Male* their ass. Now who's the cool one?[6]

---

5 Yes, there is, and you are currently looking at his/her feed.
6 Both of you!

Welp! You dug yourself into a spider hole of insecurity and there's only one way out: make your relationship official, and NAIL THAT SHIT DOWN.

Bringing up that you want to be exclusive, however, is tricky. It's not like you can betray everything you've pretended to be and just admit you aren't actually "drama-free" and "up for whatever" like your OkCupid profile says. That's why you need to broach the subject in a calm, cool, and casual way.

CASUALLY BRING UP THAT YOU WANT TO BE STRICTLY EXCLUSIVE

Every affair gets there. Every tryst trysts too far. Eventually, each relationship reaches a point where one of you says, "If you hook up with someone else, I'll drive my car into the river." But in this modern era, when everyone is bisexual and living in a polyamorous throuple, saying "Let's be exclusive" is so square. Propose a traditional monogamous relationship and maintain chill vibes by using any of the lines below!

"Are you down for Thai food tonight and also trying our hand at monogamy?"

"How should I introduce you? Friend? Buddy? Loyal-Forever-Mate? I'm cool with whatevskies."

"Can you imagine if we started dating? Ha ha, like dating dating. I absolutely can."

"I read this study that said most people have herpes and don't even know it. Guess we should probably keep the sex stuff between us!"

"Ugh, my ex is texting me. What should I say back? 'I'm in a serious, committed relationship' or . . . ?"

"I feel like we'd really be friends with benefits if we got on the same dental plan."

"What if we opened up this relationship even further by making it open to the idea of being exclusive?"

"Hey, I'm filling out a W-9 and I have a question: Would you consider me single?"

"I'm gonna have a big plate of mashed potatoes for dinner. What about you? Any side pieces you want to upgrade to the main course?"

"What do you think about seeing a movie this weekend and, I dunno, stop touching anyone but each other? That one with Mark Ruffalo looks good."

"Whoa! Schistosoma mansoni *parasitic flatworms mate for life? Maybe they know something we don't!"*

Whichever one you choose, make sure you say it word for word. All of the above have been rigorously focus-grouped for maximum effectiveness and any improvisational flourishes from you will undoubtedly ruin it.

If you've been a studious disciple of our teachings, your partner probably responded to your chill proposal with a tear-filled, "Yes. YES!" Great. Proceed to the "New Relationship" chapter for some conspicuous coupling.

NEW RELATIONSHIP

-Our Story-

We proudly announced our relationship on Facebook, only for everyone to think we were joking. I guess that's what we get for being comedians and not real people.

III.

Wow. You landed your very own *relationship*. By virtue of your wit, cunning, and hotness, you survived the uncertainty of dating. Now you may gaze down on all the lost single people from the fortress of your new relationship and say: "I know this isn't about me, but when me and *Jeff* first got together . . ."

You are no longer the lost. You are the found. And it's time to rub it in everyone's faces.

CHOOSE THE PERFECT PROFILE PICTURE FOR SOCIAL MEDIA

Now that you're official, it's time to make it *official*. Your relationship isn't real until there's a picture of you two plastered across all forms of social media. Let everyone know your shit's legit while simultaneously throwing a cold glass of lemonade in the eyes of your exes! Find a profile picture that's personal to you by choosing from one of these overplayed ideas:

- *Kissing.* Showcase your passion while staying within the confines of Facebook's strict (some would say fascist) code of conduct. A good smooch lets everybody know that you bump uglies on the regular while still keeping it PG for your aunt who shares Minion memes. It's affectionate and sweet, but also photographic evidence that you've been to first base. And if you include some subtle under-the-shirt action, it can be proof that you've gone to second base too.

- *Hiking.* Make nature about *you*. The hiking profile picture is a double whammy. Not only does it remind your single friends that you're in a relationship, it reminds them that you live a healthier lifestyle! You're outdoorsy and in-lovesy. The only downside is that you'll have to pretend to like hiking, which is essentially just walking uphill so you can look at your default desktop wallpaper.

- *Holding Hands.* Great for couples who have ugly faces but smokin' hot hands. Post a close-up of those babies intertwined and your friends will get the general idea without having to see who you settled for. Make it even more romantic with matching tattoos! Puzzle pieces, little hearts, pink and blue motorcycles with "ride or die" written in script underneath—whatever sick ink speaks to you as a couple!

- *Looking at Each Other Like You Want to Fuck in Black and White.* If you're looking for another way to put your raw sexuality on display without being reported for pornography, have sex with your eyes. It's a profile picture that says, "They clearly boned seconds later. Who took this picture?" Avoid any and all criticism by adding a black-and-white filter to make it technically art.

- *Way-Too-Close Selfie.* It's not a true couple selfie unless it's uncomfortably close. Your teeth should be so large in the frame that your dentist could identify a cavity. It's ideal for when you want to flaunt your relationship, but don't want anyone to know where you are. Recommended for prison visits and the Arby's drive-thru.

- *On Vacation.* Shirtless pics are usually frowned upon, but on vacation, all bets are off. If you're hot, this is a free pass to show off your tan, taut bodies, and disposable income all at once. You're not bragging, you're documenting your trip, and sometimes documenting your trip means sipping a margarita while your bikini-clad girlfriend sticks her ass out.

  If you're not hot, just take a picture of your initials in the sand!

- *Artsy.* Time to get creative. We're talking overexposed pictures in wheat fields, corn fields, baseball fields—any kind of field, really! Try leaning against a tree, writing "love" on your hand in marker, or kissing in a silhouette with a little light peeking through that looks like a heart. We're fans of the classic "he is looking at her but she is looking away for some reason."

- *Holding an Animal.* If the attention you get from being a couple isn't enough, you'll need to upgrade. That means having a family. Luckily, a furry dependent will qualify you as a family without having to do the work of raising a child. And if you go with a cat instead of a dog, you'll do even less work! "Look at our beautiful family! Our baby poops in a box and leaves us alone."

- *Sitting at a Restaurant with a Beer in Front of You.* This one is great for the down-to-earth couple that loves restaurants and sitting behind beer. Bonus points if it's a beer flight! Quick tip: If the bar doesn't do flights, just ask for five shot glasses and pour equal amounts of your Coors Light into each.

- *Tasteful Nudes.* Again, as long as there are no nipples or penetration (that they can see) this doesn't necessarily violate any decency agreements. You may get a comment or two from friends and family asking you to take it down because "you're embarrassing yourselves" and "this is pornography," but stay strong. A lot of people told Michelangelo to tone it down. Could you imagine the Sistine Chapel without all those soft penises?

  That being said, do not include your penis in the picture even if it is soft. Whether or not a flaccid penis should be considered sexual is not something Facebook customer service is willing to debate with you over email. And if you bring it to court, they will have better lawyers and they will countersue you for all that you're worth.

  You'll also have to start a new account, which is kind of annoying.

The social media announcement is an important step. You're not just coming out as a couple, you're coming out as a new person. Single You is dead. Long live Couple You.

SINGLE YOU VS. COUPLE YOU

Thanks to your new relationship, you're going to experience positive changes in your health, self-esteem, and how many days you can go without crying.

You spritzed some *eau de Someone Else's Approval* on your wrists and that stink of validation is following you everywhere you go. Your hollow, haunted stare has been replaced by flirtatious, fluttering lashes. You sleep soundly instead of tossing, turning, and praying for the Baba Yaga to take you in your sleep. And you shower—almost daily!

But all those subtle internal changes have external recurcussions—it's crazy how different your complexion is when you aren't dousing it nightly with your salty sadness! Couple You is a whole new breed of You. If this was the dot com bubble of the early 2000s, we'd be calling this *You 2.0*! Refer to the diagrams on the following pages to better understand your changing body.

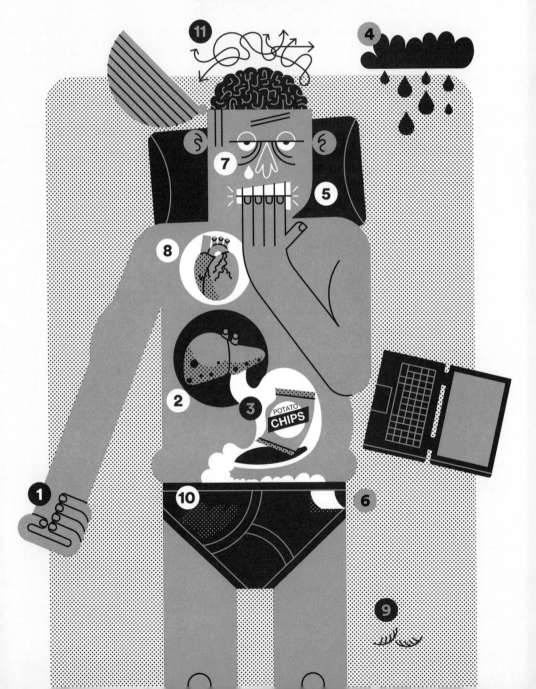

1. CARPAL TUNNEL FROM REPETITIVE MASTURBATION SO THAT HAND FORMS A PERMANENTLY CRAMPED "MASTURBATION CLAW"

2. LIVER IS CLOUDY WITH NOVELTY SHOTS LIKE "RED HEADED SLUT" AND A PILL SOMEONE TOLD YOU WAS ECSTASY BUT FELT MORE LIKE SPEED

3. STOMACH IS JUST A BAG OF POTATO CHIPS AND MORE VODKA WAITING TO BE DIGESTED

4. RAIN CLOUD

5. NAILS AND CUTICLES EATEN AWAY DURING 3 A.M. "AM I GOING TO DIE ALONE?" PANIC ATTACKS

6. UNDERWEAR IS SAME AS YESTERDAY, JUST FLIPPED INSIDE OUT, BECAUSE WHO CARES

7. BAGS UNDER YOUR EYES, FULL OF TEARS OF LONELINESS YOU HAVE CHOKED BACK

8. HEART LITERALLY DOESN'T BEAT UNLESS YOU WATCH A VIDEO ABOUT A CAT WHO WAS ADOPTED BY DOGS

9. EYELASHES ARE FALLING OFF DUE TO EATING STALE TORTILLAS WITH MAYO OVER THE SINK FOR EVERY MEAL

10. A HUMMUS STAIN FROM WHEN YOU ATE HUMMUS WITH CHOPSTICKS CAUSE YOU HAVEN'T GONE GROCERY SHOPPING SINCE YOUR LAST RELATIONSHIP AND YOU HATE YOURSELF

11. BRAIN IS A WEIRD SCRAMBLE OF REAL LIFE AND WHAT'S BEEN HAPPENING ON THE REALITY SHOWS YOU BINGE-WATCH BY YOURSELF.

    WHAT IS REALITY, EVEN? A COMPUTER SIMULATION PROBABLY.

    IS IT 4 A.M. ALREADY? GOD IT'S GETTING LATE.

    OR IS IT EARLY? IS IT 4:00 IN THE MORNING OR 4:00 IN THE AFTERNOON? IF ONLY YOU HADN'T GLUED YOUR SHADES SHUT BECAUSE THE SUNLIGHT WAS MOCKING YOUR LONELINESS.

1. HEALTHY BLUSH, LIKELY BLOOD STAGNATING IN YOUR CHEEKS FROM TOO-FREQUENT ORGASMS

2. LIVER IS LIKE A ROSY SUNSET! FROM TOO MANY SHARED CARAFES AT COZY ITALIAN *RISTORANTES*

3. STOMACH IS FULL OF SO MANY FANCY MEALS FROM RESTAURANTS! GRASS-FED STEAK AND HEIRLOOM POTATOES FROM SOME PLACE CALLED URBAN BUTCHER, BEEF TIPS FROM THAT ETHIOPIAN PLACE, A "BRUSCHETTA TRIO" . . . THAT'S RIGHT, YOU ORDER APPETIZERS NOW

4. THE POSTURE OF A SUPERMODEL BALANCING ANOTHER SUPERMODEL ON HER HEAD

5. BIRDS SIT ON YOUR SHOULDER BECAUSE YOU ATTRACT EVERYTHING GOOD AND PURE NOW

6. FRESH-BOUGHT LINGERIE ON YOUR NEWLY MOUNTAIN SPRING–SCENTED GENITALIA

7. LIPS AS RED AS THE APPLES YOU PROBABLY PICKED THIS WEEKEND, YOU ADORABLE COUPLE, YOU

8. TEETH ARE SHINY FROM OTHER PERSON'S BODILY FLUIDS. ALSO, YOU STARTED FLOSSING!

9. WALLET IS FIT AND TRIM! SEXY AND SLIM! SEE: STOMACH FULL OF FANCY RESTAURANT MEALS

10. BELLY BUTTON IS FINALLY CLEANED OUT

11. BODY HAIR IS SO WELL GROOMED YOU COULD NAB FIRST PLACE FROM THE WESTMINSTER KENNEL CLUB

12. A HUMMUS STAIN . . . BUT FROM THAT MIDDLE EASTERN RESTAURANT YOU YELPED ABOUT. YOU YELP NOW!

13. BRAIN IS STIMULATED BY ALL THE MUSEUMS YOU GO TO EVERY WEEKEND

14. BUTTHOLE IS CLEAN

COUPLE YOU

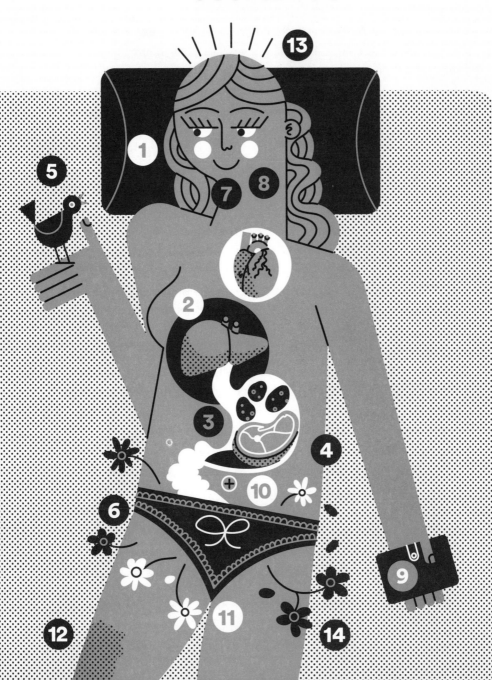

Gee, Couple You is a real catch! Maybe it's all the sex, or maybe it's because you don't eat stale tortillas over the sink anymore, but you are rocking a serious glow. And you can't be walking around with a hot new glow and think no one's going to notice. In one of life's many cruel inside jokes, everyone you have ever been romantically interested in will suddenly want to get with you.

WHAT TO DO NOW THAT EVERYONE WANTS TO BONE YOU

When you were single and ready to mingle, you were *invisingle* (invisible + single). Nobody liked you all dressed in desperation, but now that you've accessorized with the chicest of accessories—a new significant other—everyone wants a piece. It's almost like our entire generation has commitment issues and collectively wants what it can't have. Or maybe you just got really hot all of a sudden?

Suddenly, past hookups and never-acted-on flirtations all want to check in. That guy from work has magically broken up with his live-in girlfriend and wants you to come to happy hour. That girl you met in Belize is in town for the month, staying at an Airbnb down the street. You're a magnet, attracting every what-if and could've-been from the past five years. And they all want to "meet up."

News flash to all these suitors and suitettes: Too late, bitch! You're taken. Well, at least for now. This is a *new* relationship and things could always go south. It's best that you turn down these advances in a way that keeps them on the hook. As much as you're 100 percent sure, three weeks into your relationship, that this is going to last forever, it's not a bad idea to set up a Roth IRA of rebounds in case of an emergency. Get a pot on that back burner, 'cause you've got some backup stew to simmer!

So how do you turn someone down in a way that honors both the sanctity of your three-week relationship *and* the sanctity of being kind of flattered by the attention? By replying to their thirsty DMs with any of these shady, but technically-not-crossing-the-line, techniques (and corresponding examples) below:

Use the *angel emoji* in your response. The angel emoji is like a wink. It says "I'm a good girl, but underneath these heavenly robes I'm wearing the trashiest lingerie."
HIM / HER: Wow, that new profile pic is [fire emoji]
YOU: Thanks, but I'm actually in a relationship now [angel emoji]

Use an *ellipsis* to leave the door to your bedroom open *just a crack*.
HIM / HER: Hey, are you really dating Jesse now?
YOU: Yeah . . .

Send a *pouty selfie*. A selfie is inherently flirtatious. A pouty selfie is like going to first-and-a-half base electronically.
HIM / HER: [sexy selfie]
YOU: I'm dating someone, sorry! [frowning, but still sexy, selfie]

Use *temporal modifiers* like "currently" and "at the moment" and "for the time being."
HIM / HER: Hey, long time no see. What are you up to tonight?
YOU: I'm currently seeing someone at the moment so for the time being I'm off the market currently . . . [angel emoji] [frowning, but still sexy, selfie]

That should throw those horny dogs off your trail, but not so far that you can't call the horny dogs back if you need them. Definitely make sure to give the horny dogs a piece of your clothing so they know your scent and can find you again.

Unfortunately, not everyone is going to be feelin' Couple You. Believe it or not, some people are going to be *upset* that you got into a relationship and instantly changed your personality. Your social life might experience some "glowing" pains. Specifically, your relationship with your single friends.

HOW TO RELATE TO YOUR SINGLE FRIENDS NOW THAT YOU'RE AN INSUFFERABLE, HAPPY PERSON

The first time Couple You hangs out with your single friends, you'll realize that you've become an outsider. The language you once spoke fluently will begin to sound foreign: "What does *Netflix and chill* mean?" "Is *bae* a good thing?" The traditions you held dear will suddenly feel strange and empty: "Why would we go to a strip club? The drinks are so *expensive*!" "What if instead of a *Girls' Night* we did a *Girls Plus My New Boyfriend Night*?"

You've only been in a relationship for a few weeks, but already, being single is like a distant memory. The love bug bit you, then laid eggs in your ears, and rotted your brain with joy. You've become what you once hated: an insufferable, happy person.

Finding ways to relate to your single friends will be difficult now that you are obnoxiously satisfied. Their idea of fun is grabbing a drink and commiserating about their love lives, whereas yours is grabbing a drink and *bragging* about your love life. How can you relate to their frustration when you woke up to pancakes and Eskimo kisses in bed this morning? There's only one thing you can do: give unsolicited advice. Luckily, you've been in a relationship for three weeks, so you're basically a licensed couples therapist!

Whether they know it or not, every story your friends share about being single is a cry for help. Since you have everything in life—a relationship—and they have nothing—no relationship—there's no one better than you to help. If a friend talks about a problem in their love life, reassure them by explaining how you and your S.O. would handle it: "See, I feel like if Jeff wasn't texting me back right away, I would just have a conversation with him about it." There! You solved text flirting. And single people act like it's so hard!

Even if your single friends bring up something that *they* don't perceive as a problem, it's still your job to correct them. Let's say one of your friends just got out of a long-term relationship and is enjoying meeting new people and having casual sex. That may sound harmless, but as someone in a relationship, you know deep down what's best for them—being in a relationship. You are obligated to provide your sage wisdom: "That's really great that you're having fun, but sex is so much more meaningful when it's between two people who care about each other. Like me and Jeff." And now they know what kind of sex they should be having.

Think of yourself as a mother feeding her children fruits and vegetables. They might roll their eyes, but ultimately, you're giving them what they need. Speaking of fruits and vegetables, you should tell your friends lots of anecdotes about how you and Jeff just went apple-picking!

Your conversations should be less like a road trip where everyone takes a turn driving, and more like a shuttle bus where you are the bus driver and no one else can drive because you have a special license. This might mean your friends start calling you less, but honestly? Good riddance! Your calendar is packed.

YOUR INSUFFERABLY HAPPY SCHEDULE NOW THAT YOU'RE IN A NEW RELATIONSHIP

From the moment you wake yourself up by smiling too hard to when you enter a dreamless sleep because real life is better than your wildest fantasy, your day is booked solid. All that time you spent in a constant state of existential worry is now filled with "miss u" texts and sharing farm-to-table charcuterie. Your weekdays are a blur of dirty DMs at your employer's expense and passionate reunions where you act out all the filthy smut you typed. And your weekends? *Oh, your weekends!*

Your weekends are a vibrant celebration of *life*, stuffed like Christmas stockings with every event and outing you could find in *Time Out: Wherever*. The world is your oyster and you *eat oysters now*.[7] Let's take a look at a typical new couple's weekend itinerary.

---

7 At this adorable "shuck your own" spot uptown. Very off-the-beaten-path. The man who owns it is just a doll.

FRIDAY

- ☐ HAPPY HOUR COCKTAIL FLIGHTS AT SPEAKEASY YOU FOUND ON "TOP 10 DATE NOOKS" LIST
- ☐ SIX COURSE TASTING MENU AT CUTE LEBANESE VEGAN JOINT
- ☐ CHARLIE PARKER NIGHT AT JAZZ CLUB
- ☐ EAT ICE CREAM NEAR SOME FOUNTAIN FOR A WHILE
- ☐ AFTER-HOURS STARGAZING AT MUSEUM OF NATURAL HISTORY
- ☐ TACOS AT FOOD TRUCK WITH LONGEST LINE
- ☐ NIGHTCAP AT BAR YOU FOUND ON "TOP 10 DIVE BARS WITHOUT DANGEROUS LOCALS"
- ☐ WALK HOME, TAKING ROUTE THAT GOES OVER BRIDGE WITH THE GOOD VIEWS
- ☐ HAVE SEX FOUR TIMES

SATURDAY

- ☐ WAKE UP IN THEIR BED, TRACE NAMES OF FUTURE CHILDREN ON THEIR PERFECT CHEEK
- ☐ HAVE SEX FOUR TIMES
- ☐ PICK BLUEBERRIES, MAKE BLUEBERRY PANCAKES FROM SCRATCH
- ☐ APPALACHIAN BIKE TOUR
- ☐ PICNIC BRUNCH IN PAGODA UNDER CHERRY BLOSSOMS AT BOTANICAL GARDEN
- ☐ MUSEUM OF MEDIEVAL TAPESTRY
- ☐ SUDANESE FILM FESTIVAL
- ☐ DINNER AT RAMEN SUPPER CLUB YOU FOUND ON "TOP 10 SECRET RESTAURANTS THAT ARE JUST A DUDE'S HOUSE" LIST
- ☐ TANGO LESSONS AND TAPAS SPREAD
- ☐ DESSERT IN AMTRAK DINING CAR HEADING UPSTATE
- ☐ BEACH BONFIRE

- [ ] KARAOKE AT BAR YOU FOUND ON "TOP 10 BARS RUINED BY KARAOKE" LIST
- [ ] NIGHTCAP IN AMTRAK DINING CAR HEADING DOWNSTATE
- [ ] WALK HOME SHOELESS IN THE RAIN
- [ ] WATCH WORKERS CLOSE UP SHOP FOR THE NIGHT AND CONDESCENDINGLY REFLECT UPON THEIR QUAINT LIVES
- [ ] HAVE SEX FOUR TIMES

SUNDAY

- [ ] WAKE UP HUMMING THE SONG YOU ARE GOING TO WALK DOWN THE AISLE TO
- [ ] HAVE SEX FOUR TIMES
- [ ] BREAKFAST GYROS AT MICHELIN-RATED DELI
- [ ] HIKE TRAIL YOU FOUND ON "TOP 10 URBAN TRUDGES" LIST
- [ ] JET SKI WITH THE DOLPHINS™ EXPERIENCE
- [ ] WINE TASTING IN ANOTHER STATE
- [ ] KIMCHI FESTIVAL
- [ ] HELICOPTER WITH THE EAGLES™ EXPERIENCE
- [ ] APPLY FOR LOAN TO SUSTAIN EXPENSIVE NEW LIFESTYLE
- [ ] BULGARIAN PRIDE PARADE
- [ ] ARTISANAL BEER SHAKES AT COLD STONE BREWERY YOU FOUND ON "TOP 10 BAD IDEAS" LIST
- [ ] DOUBLE DATE AT LITTLE BURGER JOINT INSIDE BANK WITH FRIEND FROM WORK
- [ ] AFTER DARK SURF LESSONS
- [ ] HORSE-DRAWN CARRIAGE HOME
- [ ] WATCH TWO SEASONS OF *CHEERS*
- [ ] HAVE SEX FOUR TIMES

Soon, your significant other will add an even more exciting event to the itinerary: They will ask you to be their date to a friend's wedding. The good news? Your partner is not terrified of the idea of juxtaposing you and nuptials! The bad news? Everything else.

You are going to be surrounded by your S.O.'s friends. And unlike your friends, they have zero history with you and no obligation to listen to your apple-picking stories. You are an outsider. An accessory. An extra warm body that's been hovering around. You are a +1.

HOW TO SURVIVE BEING A +1 AT A WEDDING
A DRINKING GAME

There will be no greater test for your future as a couple than attending a wedding as a +1, especially if your S.O. is in the wedding party. You're in for a night of inside jokes that you don't understand, tearful declarations of love between people you don't give a shit about, and wondering whether or not your partner is ever going to be done taking pictures. On top of that, you can't act like an asshole, because you're surrounded by your S.O.'s friends, aka judgmental strangers who have your partner's ear and could potentially call for you to be dumped. As a +1, you are the Away Team.

Usually when you hang out with their friends, you at least have your S.O. as a buffer. Not the case at a stranger's wedding. While your partner is off sharing pre-ceremony drinks in the bride's or groom's suite, you're left to fend for yourself. The best way to get through the night is to drink yourself blind. That's why we've created a +1 Drinking Game! It requires drinking in church, so remember to bring a flask.

DRINK if your partner ditches you to ride in a limo with the wedding party while you sit in the back of a rinky shuttle full of strangers.

DRINK if your partner was invited to a bridal-party-only pregame and you're stuck sitting in a pew for a full hour before the ceremony starts.

DRINK if a member of the bride's or groom's family introduces themselves, you try to explain who you are, then you both silently acknowledge you don't need to talk to each other.

DRINK if you have to watch your partner walk down the aisle linking arms with some stranger who is hotter than you.

DRINK for every aunt's gasp when the bride appears.

DRINK anytime the clergy quotes a weirdly sexist Bible verse or mentions Hell.

DRINK every minute that passes as you try to track down your partner during the cocktail hour.

DRINK every time you look at your phone because it is your only friend (besides booze).

DRINK if the Maid of Honor's toast is a heavily scripted sob session complete with furiously shaking script.

DRINK   if the Best Man roasts the groom with inside jokes that are so deep, he might as well be speaking a foreign language.

DRINK   if their friends put on some kind of heartfelt performance, like a song, dance, or improv routine that makes the bride or groom cry but makes you consider hanging yourself with the table runner.

DRINK   if your partner awkwardly insists that you be in a picture even though no one else cares that you are there.

DRINK   if your partner asks you to slow down, but you don't listen because you wouldn't be drinking if they hadn't ditched you in the first place.

DRINK   some water if your partner apologizes and promises to take you to Taco Bell on the way home.

MAINLINE HEROIN   if you find out that there is an after-party and your partner really wants to go.

With the fresh stink of love in the air and all that booze in your veins, you won't be able to help but reflect on your own relationship. Where it's going. Where it's been. When it started.

Hey, when did it start, anyway?

COBBLE TOGETHER AN ANNIVERSARY OUT
OF YOUR AMORPHOUS BEGINNINGS

It used to be that a relationship began when a Stand-Up Kinda Guy gave his Letterman Jacket to his Favorite Gal. Back then, sharing a milkshake was like third base. Now you have to do butt stuff just to keep up!

There are no more fairytale romances, not even in Disney movies (what up to my strong ladies in *Frozen*). Courtship has a lot less serenading with lutes, and a lot more cunnilingus to Drake. "Going steady" has been replaced with "trying to pretend you don't like them by continuing to date other people." Then one day, after several confusing months competing for the upper hand, you realize you have become a couple. So . . . what is your anniversary? Let's comb through your history.

Should it be your first date? Most likely your first date was a blurry month of "come over and watch Hulu" until one of you nutted up and went for a genital. Even if you did have a clear-cut first date, it was likely set up on Bumble or whatever dating app came out in the three seconds since you've turned to this page. Do you really want to celebrate the time you went to a well-lit bar with a stranger and had three of your friends on call in case he was a serial killer?

What about the first time you kissed? Kissing is too low stakes. Considering you were probably wasted, in the middle of the street, being cheered on by drunk college kids, this isn't the best choice. You may have even made out with somebody else that night. Is it your anniversary with them too? That's twice as many presents to buy!

The first time you had sex? If you made love like a teen couple in a rom-com on prom night, sure. But chances are you bought condoms from a bodega at 1 A.M., then got busy on the floor because your bed was too creaky and you didn't want to wake your roommate up. First hookups are unglamorous shit-shows that need not be relived with a Hallmark card.

When you became exclusive? Wow, you're writing your own Nicholas Sparks movie here! "She knew Dennis was the one the moment, in the pouring rain, he agreed to stop banging his ex." In case you didn't smell the stink of sarcasm on our breath, there's nothing romantic about this. Good luck explaining it to the maître d' as he pours your vintage Moët & Chandon: "Are you celebrating your wedding?" "No, we're celebrating not having to get STD tests anymore."

The first time one of you slipped up and called the other "boyfriend" or "girlfriend" during an introduction? Now you're thinking in the right direction! One of you accidentally says the G- or the B-word then, immediately, catches the other person's eye. A blush in both of your cheeks. The moment passes, uncorrected. Suddenly, a new stage is solidified. The whisper of the future is warm on the back of your necks. Until the next day, when they introduce you to their friend from college as "that Craigslist girl I bought an air conditioner from."

First time you used them as an emergency contact? This could work, but only if you're doing it for the right reasons. Listing someone as your emergency contact is meaningful if they are truly the person you trust most when things go wrong. It doesn't mean much if you're just looking for someone who isn't your mom to be the first person they call when you pass out at the gynecologist after they tell you you have gonorrhea.

The first time your parents let you sleep in the same bed? Trick question, you're going to do it anyway. Or you're not coming home for Thanksgiving. Watch me, Mom.

The first time you see each other naked in a nonsexual context? Now this is a relationship benchmark. A magical time when braless boobs flap in the open air. When fat folds can be their foldiest. When you can reach under the coffee table wearing only your socks and you just don't give a shit that your ass looks pasty. Yes, the first time you truly stop trying to impress each other is the perfect day to mark the beginning of the rest of your lives together. It's a beautiful combination of romantic and a little sad.

How about the first time you take a shit at their place? This is also a pretty good one.

Wow, things have gotten pretty serious since you pinched that fateful deuce at their apartment. It might be time to drop the "new" from "new relationship." Heck, it might be time to turn the gas off your back burner and transfer your backup stew to some Tupperware (remember the backup stew joke?).

But before you enter the doorway to the next phase of your relationship, you'll need the password. A familiar phrase, uttered by one or both of you. Three measly syllables that you've said all your life, and yet, suddenly, fill you with dread: "I Love You." Wow, even typing that was an act of bravery. That's why you need to make sure you . . .

You might be thinking, "Life is too short to not say how I feel!" Well, is life too short to be REJECTED!? Is it too short to freak out your significant other by moving too fast? *No.* Life is long and tedious with plenty of time to agonize over past mistakes. Go out on a limb, and it's bound to snap.

But, what if I love them? That's a good thing! So long as you keep your mouth shut and don't mutter a fucking word about it. If you can't keep the L-word out of your naive, sentimental trap, tiptoe around it without actually saying it. Phrases like, "I *might* be falling in love with you . . ." or "I feel like we *could* fall in love some day," set up a nice, cushy landing so they feel comfortable enough to take the plunge. Because you sure as hell aren't!

Isn't that kind of manipulative? No. It's getting the other person to do what you want them to do without asking. Very different.

What if I accidentally say it? Hastily tack "rope" at the end of it. "I love you! . . . rope! Europe. I love Europe." If your significant other is curious as to why you brought up a continent at a romantic moment, remind them that France is very romantic, then pivot to a polite conversation about how much you enjoy cathedrals and cobbled streets.

If it happens at the height of physical pleasure, add someone else's name at the end. "I love you! . . . Bill." They will be so distracted by your betrayal, that the dreaded L-word won't even enter the post-sex discussion.

Can I say it in another language? Interesting loophole. Yes, as long as the language is as far removed from your native tongue as possible. If you speak Spanish, don't say it in Italian. *Ti amo* is too similar to *te amo*, so you run the risk of getting called out and having to fake a stroke. Instead, try a simple Mandarin *Wŏ ài nĭ*, a wordy Javanese *kulo tresno marang panjenenganor*, or a hearty Norwegian *jeg elsker deg*. You will have the satisfaction of speaking your truth, but to them, you will just be saying nonsense and/or having another stroke. Be mindful of what language they learned in high school or if they studied abroad. You don't want some Javanese Rhodes Scholar telling you *Iki obah cepet banget*.[8]

OK, how do I get them to say it so I can tell them how I feel already? You don't want to go first, but you also don't want to wait around for them to nut up and do it. That's why you must *bait* your significant other, with one of our patented *Master Baits*:

- Put them in a position where they *have* to blurt it out. At a time when they're running really late for a business trip to another state or country, give a long, nervous, meandering speech about your feelings: "I've got really strong feelings for you . . . and I've never said this to anyone but . . . oh boy! This is so hard. I guess it all started when my father withheld affection from me as a child . . ." Eventually they'll have to blurt it out or they'll miss their flight.

- Text "I love you." When they respond with "I love you too," respond with, "Sorry, that was for my mom. YOU LOVE ME!?" Sure, you technically said it first, but it was an "accident." They said it for real!

---

8 "This is moving too fast."

- Shout "you never loved me anyway!" during a fight. They'll have no choice but to respond with, "Of course I love you!" Plus, it'll distract them from whatever you did to piss them off!

Fine. Once they've said it, then I can say it? Not right away. Make 'em sweat. Change the subject in a way that makes it unclear if you didn't hear it, or you're purposefully ignoring it. They'll go through the wringer, wondering but not knowing, until they eventually decide the only way to find out is to say it again. The second time they say it, let that L-word fly! Take two, give one back. It will be nice to share how you feel, but even nicer to know that for the rest of the relationship, the "I love you" tally will be tipped in your favor.

Only a monster would withhold affection like this. First, not a question. Second, yes, but, like, a *scared* monster. Like how they say sharks are more afraid of you than you are of them.
I don't think they say that about sharks.

Which one of you said "I love you" first? Neither. We're still holding out. Murph will only go as far as "I *think* I could fall in love with you . . ." and Emily keeps calling him Bill in bed.

And with that, you're ready to say those other three magic words: Long-Term Relationship.

LONG-TERM RELATIONSHIP

-Our Story-

We were already married by the time
we would be considered a long-term
relationship. But don't worry! Everyone
moves at their own pace. We just happened
to move at a reckless, irresponsible one.

IV.

So, you've reached the precise ratio of sexual to nonsexual nudity to be considered a Long-Term Relationship.[9] Your flashy sports car has transformed into a reliable sedan. It's not as exciting but, good news, it probably won't kill you either. You no longer have to try to impress your significant other because you've earned your relationship tenure. It is officially easier to stay with you than to break up with you. How romantic!

The beginning of a relationship is like a peacock flaunting its feathers in everyone's face. Somewhere around month three or four, though, the feathers fall off, and you're just a big, shitty, naked bird. This is a time when passions wane and are replaced with things like logistics and obligations and quietly reading on a couch next to each other sometimes. But if done right, a Long-Term Relationship is more fun than a new one. Farting is allowed, you don't have to make plans on the weekends, and you can stop pretending that you enjoy having sex standing up. That's right: *you can finally stop showing off in bed*.

---

9   Or, if you work from home, 1:11.

STOP MESSING AROUND WITH FLASHY SEXUAL POSITIONS AND SETTLE ON THE TWO YOU LIKE

When you first hook up with someone, you set an unrealistic standard of sex. Your lovemaking is a flurry of athletic feats that would give an Olympic gymnast a cramp. But once the three- to six-month-long adrenaline boner wears off, you start to realize: having sex on the kitchen table isn't hot, it just hurts. Wouldn't it be nice to just do it in a goddamn bed?

You probably have a go-to sexual position that you enjoy but stray from to seem adventurous. For many people, this might be Missionary. Missionary gets a bad rap because it's named after churches who go to Third World countries and give Bibles to people who need food. Not only is it misguided, it's unsexy! Besides the occasional "Oh God" or "Christ, yes, pour that candle wax in my butthole," religion has no place in the bedroom.

When you picture Missionary sex, you probably imagine two virgins apologizing to each other in their marriage bed. But Missionary is what you make of it. Yes, it is a staple of doughy dudes who last three pumps and then pass out on top of their girlfriends, but it's also a staple of porn stars, who perform it with sexy, arched backs while covered in lube for hours on end. Though those two scenarios are technically the same position, there is a distinct difference between *Prematurely Ejaculating for Jesus* and *Taking the Direct Route to Poundtown*. And there is nothing wrong with an efficient commute to Poundtown.

Provided that it is performed as sexily as you can sex, Missionary is a position that you should keep in your repertoire. It's comfortable, it provides full view of the goods, and it is simple enough that you can really make it your own. Ladies, try looking him in the eye or, better yet, pull him on top of you and pretend he's someone else! Fellas, enjoy the sight of bouncing boobs or bouncing eyes if you're a gentleman!

While Missionary is a clear winner, it's important to spread the workload. That's why we also recommend Cowgirl. Cowgirl boasts all of the advantages of Missionary, but puts the woman in the driver's seat. It even has a cool costume associated with it, available at any number of fine Party City locations! As feminists who seek equality both in and out of the bedroom, we believe it is essential that women sometimes take the dominant position and pound that peen with authority.

You can, of course, sprinkle in a little Doggy Style when you're feeling adventurous. *Kneeling* doggy style, of course. We recommend you retire Standing Doggy Style. Very few activities are made more enjoyable by standing. That's doubly true for standing *and* lifting. If you're curious about more athletic positions, like Standing Jackhammer, try furiously slamming a medicine ball into your crotch at a CrossFit class instead. It'll be just as difficult and just as pleasurable!

In addition to Jackhammer and Standing Doggy Style, you can also retire the following positions: Wheelbarrow, Reverse Wheelbarrow, Standing Tiger, Froggy Style, The Passion Pretzel, Piledriver, Suspended Congress, Churning the Butter, Making Snow Angels, Sporking, the Organ Grinder, and anything else that involves spinning, *pranayama* breathing, creatine supplements, or getting rug burn on your ass. There is a time and place for exercise and it is not while you're jizzing. Sex is not a touchdown dance. Sex is *the touchdown itself*. So stop showing off and just enjoy scoring.

Unfortunately, this won't be the only way your sex life will change. Not only will you stop wanting to do it Reverse Piledriver–style—some nights you won't want to do it *at all*. Everyone likes the idea of having sex three times a day, but the genital-chapping reality is that our bodies were not built for it. If your vagina feels like it's been in a rugby scrum at the end of the day, or your penis is ejaculating teaspoons of dust, it's probably time to transition to a more reasonable schedule.

However, your healthier, more refined sexual appetite might cause some early complications. Namely, disagreements. Sex is a shortcut to forgiveness, and without it, minor squabbles you once swept under the rug with a good rub and tug will become full-fledged fights.

But that's OK! Fighting is healthy. If you don't occasionally disagree with your partner, you are probably a concubine, or at best, a sister wife. Any relationship that values equality over maximum number of heirs, however, will eventually encounter differing opinions. When this happens, take a deep breath. Make sure you don't take your anger out on anything of value. Like your partner's heart! Or an antique lamp.

TAKE OUT YOUR ANGER RESPONSIBLY
AN INVENTORY OF WHAT IS AND WHAT ISN'T OK TO THROW DURING A FIGHT

Maybe you'll talk it out. Maybe talking won't suffice, so you'll yell it out. Maybe yelling will become redundant as, over time, you grow numb to the volume and tenor of each other's ire. When this happens, you'll find yourself looking for new ways to express your frustration. You might up the ante by threatening to go for a long walk by yourself down a dangerous street in the middle of the night, but more likely you'll just throw something.

Sham pillows, pool noodles, an unopened family pack of toilet paper—all of these are well suited for flights of rage. A beloved family heirloom, a picture frame of the two of you during happier times, their wide-screen TV—these items are *not* intended for airborne voyage, mainly because they require an additional apology or financial reimbursement after you have reconciled. No one wants to apologize to begin with, so why add something else to the list?

Since it may be difficult to pick the perfect projectile in the moment, refer to our list of *Acceptable* and *Unacceptable* items to throw:

- ***Pillows and Stuffed Animals.*** Anything soft, filled with something softer, is *Acceptable*. This includes duvet covers, couch cushions, uncooked empanadas, and a sleeping bag full of whipped cream.

- ***Furniture.*** Chairs, tables, armoires, and chaise lounges are *Unacceptable*. Beanbag chairs and unstrung hammocks, however, are *Acceptable*. And if you're living right, you should have plenty of those! We sleep in a novelty beanbag that looks like a baked potato.

- ***Cleaning Supplies.*** Paper towels and old rags are definitely *Acceptable*. Bleach, insect poison, and Drano are *Unacceptable*. You don't want to blind someone over an argument about whether or not "irregardless" is a word.

- ***Food.*** It may seem like this is an obvious *Unacceptable*, but there are actually quite a few exceptions. If you threw a single-serving package of yogurt and it splattered against the wall with a ridiculous *plop!* that might be pretty funny and worth the cleanup.

A pineapple, however, can kill a man. Avoid hard foods like unripe avocados in favor of soft foods like ripe avocados.

- **Beverages.** *Unacceptable*. Especially in frozen and boiling form. Even water. Water may not stain carpet, but it does make mascara run and curl recently straightened hair. You don't want to piss off someone holding a piping-hot flat iron.

- **Balls.** Most are *Acceptable*, even encouraged, due to the fact that your argument might turn into a game of catch. Bouncy balls, racquetballs, and jai alai pelotas, however, are *Unacceptable*. Once those things get going, it's hard to stop 'em!

- **Whatever's On Your Desk.** Chucking that porcelain Buddha you bought when you tried to get into meditation is *Unacceptable*. What are you, writing an O. Henry story here? The weight of all that dramatic irony is gonna break a window. However, if your desk is covered in papers, it might be fun to make it snow dental bills.

- **Musical Instruments.** *Unacceptable*, unless it is a ukulele. Any grown-ass adult who plays the ukulele deserves to have their ukulele destroyed.

- **A Plastic Bag or a Feather Boa.** Technically *Acceptable*, but be warned: They will fly away and you will look stupid.

- **Your Voice.** This is impressive if you can do it. *Acceptable*.

After a heated argument, your confidence in the relationship will be shattered—along with all the ukuleles and ripe avocados you've hurled at each other. But this is only a tiny step back in your otherwise forward march to neighboring graves (cute!). Instead of breaking up over every problem and entertaining every insecurity, you've got to be more mature. You're in a long-term relationship now. It's time to grow up.

ESTABLISHING HEALTHY BOUNDARIES AND TRUST
(UNLESS THEY LEAVE THEIR EMAIL OPEN)

Trust issues are a self-fulfilling prophecy. If you refuse to let someone in because you're afraid of getting hurt, you'll push them away, which will lead to them 69-ing some stranger at their work convention in Milwaukee.[10] People tend to live up to our expectations of them—whether you treat your S.O. like a faithful partner or a sociopath bent on collecting genital warts, they're likely to fill the role. You've been in this relationship for several months now, and you can't move forward without making yourself vulnerable. You have to be able to trust your partner.

Unless they, like, leave their phone unlocked while they're taking a long shower.

You can't fall in love unless you allow yourself to fall *all the way*. Or, at least *almost* all the way. Like just short of not picking up their unlocked phone so you can take a quick peek at their alerts. If they didn't want you to look at it, they wouldn't have just left it sitting there.

---

10 Using the mutually fulfilling 69 techniques we taught you, no doubt!

And you can see their push notifications without scrolling through anything, so no harm, no foul. Again, you trust them. It's not snooping if you're still on the home screen.

Show your partner the same courtesy they have shown you. A relationship cannot succeed with double standards. If you can go out with your friends, why interrogate them when they go out with theirs? If they don't wait up for you, why do you wait up for them? If you would never leave your phone just sitting there unlocked, why did they? They must have nothing to hide. Consent to browse is implied.

By keeping your guard up, you limit the risk of getting hurt—but you also limit your chances of finding happiness. In the end, the risk is what makes it worth it. Speaking of risk, they probably aren't going to be in that shower much longer, so go ahead and do a quick word search in their text history for the first name of that cutie they work with. Again, love is about letting yourself be vulnerable, and what is more vulnerable than a phone without a passcode?

You will have moments of weakness. Be upfront about your feelings. Rather than burying your insecurity and harboring resentment, have a conversation. Chances are, whatever you're suspicious about has an easy explanation and you can both have a laugh about it. Like this "happy birthday" text they got from that cute coworker you just discovered while going full Snowden on their phone. At least, they *better* have an explanation! And it better be fucking funny!

Honesty is a two way street. If you admit that you found the offending birthday text, and *winky-face emoji*, by borderline hacking their phone, you're depriving them of the opportunity to be honest with *you*. Instead, set up an elaborate trap, wherein you pretend that you've been getting flirty texts from *your* hot coworkers to see if they confess to getting flirty texts from theirs. If they don't fess up, they no longer have the moral high ground, and you can freely accost them for lying! Their betrayal of *your* trust was way worse than your betrayal of *their* trust. And relationships are all about trust.

...

Two minutes of snooping on someone's phone could fuel a lifetime of jealousy. Try fueling something positive instead!

CHANNEL YOUR JEALOUSY INTO PRODUCTIVE ACTIVITIES

We all know jealousy is toxic. But knowing that something's bad for you doesn't stop you from ordering it at the drive-thru at 3 A.M.! Since you can't always reason your way out of it, try taking that nervous energy and putting it into one of these productive hobbies!

- *Running.* Exercise is a good way to burn up that bad energy. Going out for a daily jog can help you cultivate peace of mind (and killer buns!). Choose a route that challenges you, but also goes past the bar your significant other said they were going to after work. If that "runner's high" doesn't calm you down, doing a lap around the bar to make sure they weren't lying to you will.

- *Music.* Learning how to sing or play an instrument will allow you to process your emotions through song! It's also a great excuse to buy a bunch of recording equipment, which you can use to bug their car.

- ***Bird-Watching.*** Yellow-throated sparrows, belted kingfishers, red-breasted nuthatches—the world of birds is truly fascinating! Bird-watching requires a Zen-like patience that will transfer into other aspects of your life. Of course, you'll need to invest in a good pair of binoculars, and maybe learn how to climb the telephone pole outside your significant other's apartment. Since when is looking at something through binoculars "spying"? You don't hear the birds complaining!

- ***Painting.*** Art is a powerful form of therapy! That's why we recommend painting. Specifically, your face, in camouflage. That way you can hide in the bushes and surprise your significant other when they get home from the business mixer you weren't invited to.

- ***Fashion.*** Find some fabric and *play*. You're gonna need a suit of twigs and grass to match the camouflage.

- ***Performance Art.*** Avant-garde performers never shy away from the grotesque or the absurd. Nor should you, as you make *absurd* accusations about your significant other and the *grotesque* person they are sitting next to at the gastropub you just barged into. If it's pathetic and uncomfortable for everyone involved, it's supposed to be. That's performance art.

- ***Poetry.*** Maybe they'll forgive you if you write a really heartfelt poem.

Once you've made amends, the two of you can become a more mature couple. This is one of the joys of a Long-Term Relationship. You replace crazy patterns of behavior, like jealousy and clinginess, with more sustainable patterns of behavior, like "just kind of caring less." There's no need to play games anymore. You're in it for the long haul. You can stop worshiping the idea of each other and start loving each other for who you really are: total weirdos.

Let your skeletons out of the closet and introduce those bony dudes to your S.O.!

THINGS YOU CAN ADMIT YOU LIKE NOW

In the beginning, you only emphasized the hobbies and interests that made you sound cool, unique, and fuckable. You told them you were getting into boxing and wouldn't shut up about that one time you went surfing. You came across as idiosyncratic and a breath of fresh air as you confessed your love for underground hip-hop and thrift-store shopping. You acted like you were *such a nerd* for being into graphic novels, like universally beloved and blockbuster-adapted *Watchmen*.

There are two types of weird: cool weird and *weird* weird. There's "Yeah I'm pretty weird, I like to people watch," and then there's "Yeah, I'm pretty weird, I like to put my finger in my belly button then sniff it." The beginning of a relationship is all about *cool* weird. The rest of your life, however, will be *weird* weird. You are free to be dorky, disgusting, lame, lazy, and honest about the fact that your favorite vacation spot is Disney World. And guess what? They're going to love you more for it! Or at the very least, pretend they didn't hear you.

The following is a list of things you can finally admit you like:

- going to bed early
- farting
- the movies of Anne Hathaway
- feet, in a sexual way
- pro wrestling
- lip-sync videos
- Magic: The Gathering
- peeing in pools
- Justin Timberlake's disco phase
- *World of Warcraft*
- *CSI: Las Vegas*
- blowing snot rockets in the shower
- cargo shorts
- man beanies
- Matchbox Twenty
- the way your armpits smell after Pilates
- gas station hot dogs
- anime (the regular kind)
- anime (the weird kind)
- *Grey's Anatomy*
- a thumb up the butt
- doing word searches
- duct tape wallets
- LARPing
- steampunk
- healing crystals

- swing dancing
- ska
- frozen yogurt
- calling frozen yogurt "froyo"
- reality TV
- Starbucks
- watching people play Dungeons & Dragons on YouTube
- getting peed on

As you dispel any illusion that you are even remotely *cool*, you might as well add *healthy, cultured,* or *intellectual* to the bonfire.

THINGS YOU CAN ADMIT YOU DON'T LIKE

At the start of the relationship, you were as active as a couple in a herpes commercial. You were running on the fumes of a budding love, and spent your precious weekends going on excursions and picnicking. But the novelty's worn off and you want your Sundays back. That's OK! This is the beauty of being in a Long-Term Relationship. You don't have to do *anything*.

You can stop pretending you like to go on hikes. *No longer* will you waste prime brunch hours on a dusty uphill walk. *Never again* will you say something like "the air just tastes better up here." *Nary* another picture of a skyline shall be taken and later deleted, because honestly, what are you supposed to do with a picture of a skyline?

You can stop pretending you like museums. Contemporary museums, natural history museums, even museums that are desperately trying to seem cool (we're looking at you, Museums of Sex and Torture). It won't matter if it's First Friday or Last Sunday or if that thing's free all year round, you can just admit you have zero interest in whispering in a room full of strangers. Unless there's a rain room, cause, holy shit, think of the 'grams.

You can stop pretending you want to go apple picking or pumpkin patching or truffle foraging or any other activity that we, as modern people with access to grocery stores, don't actually have to do anymore. Actually, truffle foraging would be pretty cool because you'd get to hang out with a pig.

You can stop pretending you like anything that requires more than forty-five minutes to get to, but doesn't involve staying overnight. This includes, but is not limited to, aquariums, arboretums, sites of historical battles, and big statues in the middle of nowhere. A notable exception would be theme parks, which are arguably worth it.

You can stop pretending you like jazz or classical or any live music that you're expected to sit down and watch. It's music, dude. Either you're elbowing some guy named Thrasher mid-mosh, or you can just listen to it on headphones.

After months of packed weekends, you can relax and just admit: sometimes the best activity is no activity. Unless you've been writing a book with your significant other and haven't left the apartment or seen another human being in two and a half months. In which case, First Friday at the arboretum two hours away, here we come!

All this *being you* and *letting your freak flag fly* is great. Except when anyone outside of your sick twosome has to witness it.

PET NAMES YOU SHOULD NEVER SAY IN PUBLIC

When you are in a relationship, you develop a language that only you understand. If they text "Wanna get stinky with pinky?" you'll know they mean "Would you like to go to our favorite Florribean restaurant, Pink Flamingo, and get the BBQ shrimp fritters that always give you gas?" It's like being part of a secret society! Which is secret because no one else wants to be in it.

Then come the nicknames, which are forever evolving. After months of spending all your time together, what started as "Matty" will have morphed into something hideous like "Matty Watty Boo" or even something incomprehensible, like "Matty Mac Daddy the BeBoppin' Caddy." These nicknames will be born of inside jokes, fond memories, and playful affection, but to someone else's ears, they might as well be born in Hell.

There are a few terms of endearment that are chill to let loose in public: babe, hon, and boo. That's about it. Anything else will elicit so much disgust that you might as well shoot a snot rocket in someone's cola. On the following pages, we've compiled a list of cutesy word crimes you should never let slip past your teeth.

- *Anything food based.*

  Pumpkin, Peanut, Sugar, Bean, Muffin, Honey Cakes, Tater Tot, Squash Blossom, and Ketchup Packet are off limits. Your friends do not want to picture you making "nom nom" sounds while you affectionately pretend to bite their elbow.

- *Anything that ends in -y or -ie.*

  Baby, Lovey, Sweetie, Cutie, Poopsie, Fatty, Grumpy, Sneezy, and Lumpy are all too cutesy. It's like tar-and-feathering your audience, but with honey and lace doilies.

- *Anything preceded by "Hot."*

  Hot Stuff, Hot Lips, Hot Ass, Hot Tits, Hot Potato, Hot Toddy, Hot Dog, Hot Pocket, and Hot-Plate-Be-Careful-Let-It-Cool-Down-Before-You-Touch-It are a steamin' heap of nope. Go ahead and drop "hot" from your vocabulary unless you are talking about the weather in Tucson or doing an ironic nod to 2003's very own Paris Hilton.

- *Anything involving the word "Snuggle" or "Cuddle."*

  Snuggle Bear, Snuggle Boo, Cuddle Biddy, Snuggle Poo, and Cuddley Wuddley Snuggle Bun will lose you at least three to five friends the moment you utter it. Once said, it cannot be unsaid. Cuddle Biddy will forever stain the way your peers see you, destroying personal and professional relationships alike. Do not be the person overheard talking to Cuddle Biddy on the phone at work.

- **Anything in a foreign language you don't speak.**
  Bella, Bambino, Mon Amor, Mon Cherie, and Bellissimo are a big fat *nyet/nein/non/ne*. If you can't order off a menu in that language without pointing, you can't use it to get laid.

- **Anything you've seen in a 1950s movie.**
  Sweetheart, Darling, Dear, and Dearest belong to grandparents, Hitchcock films, and suburban dads at a restaurant with a cute waitress. Unless you want to evoke a father of three low-key sexually harassing a young waitress, we'd advise you stick to "babe."

- **Any combination of the aforementioned.**
  Honey Bean, Pumpkin Baby, Sugar Poopsie, Bunny Muffin, Harlequin Fatty, Hot Peanut, and Mon Ketchup are all unforgivable word sins that, if spoken in the company of non–significant others, will result in your swift and total social ostracizing.

Pet names are wonderful—so long as no one else has to hear them. We know you really want to use Mon Ketchup, but please do so in the privacy of your own home. Speaking of which, it might be time to upgrade Mon Ketchup to Mon . . . Roommate.

MOVING IN TOGETHER

–Our Story–

We spent months trying to find the perfect apartment . . . and boy did we! A one bedroom with a bay window on a tree-lined street in the heart of Brooklyn with a steep broker's fee that we immediately had to forfeit because our jobs moved to L.A. Now we live in a first-floor apartment and old people look in our windows.

V.

Moving in together is like saying, "We're interested in marriage, can we test drive it?" You survived the ups and downs of Lust and Love, now let's see how you handle the final *L*: Logistics.

BREAKDOWN OF EACH ⌐ IN EVERY STAGE OF YOUR RELATIONSHIP

- ▉ LUST
- ▢ LOVE
- ▢ LOGISTICS

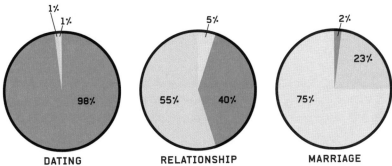

DATING   RELATIONSHIP   MARRIAGE

As time moves on, that sweet slice of Logistics pie is only going to get fatter and carb-ier. That's why we're vocal advocates of not only sleeping together before you get married, but actually living together too. *Why buy the cow when you're getting the milk for free?* More like, *Why buy the cow if you don't know how the cow handles everyday stresses like paying the gas bill or remembering to call the plumber?*

There's no magic equation that's going to tell you when to move in together. There is, however, a flowchart!

SHOULD YOU MOVE IN TOGETHER?

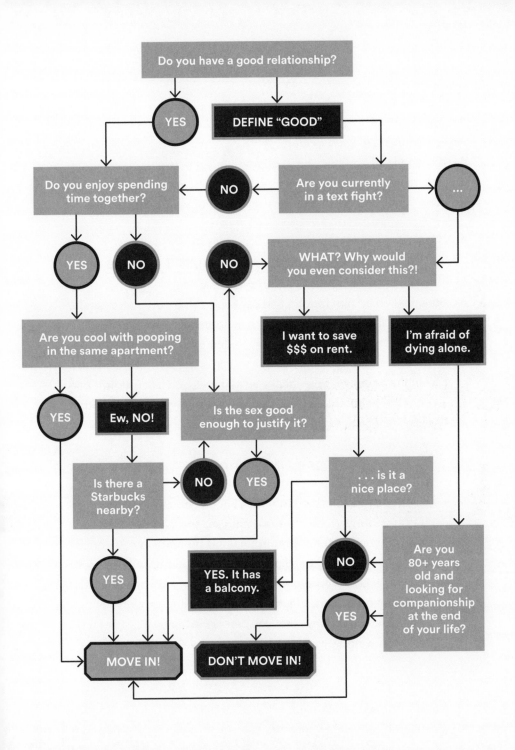

If you landed on *Don't Move In!*, too bad. Enjoy all the "I swear this is the last time" sex you guys are going to have over the next few months as you break up in slow motion.

If you landed on *Move In!*—congrats! Buy a bottle of champagne, but maybe a cheap one. Moving is expensive. However, there is a way to save money *and* challenge the very fabric of your relationship.

TEST THE RELATIONSHIP BY NOT HIRING MOVERS

Sure, you could hire movers and save yourself a buttload of strain, both physical and emotional. But why hide from the inevitable? The two of you are going to have to learn how to deal with stress as a unified, cooperative team, so you might as well do it in one weekend of pure hell.

Moving is a *breeze*. Specifically, one that is so strong that it can tear one of those inflatable tube men you see at car dealerships from its base. All you have to do is . . .

1. Pack everything you own into boxes, which you have to also buy, in addition to bubble wrap.
2. Break your back hauling them to your car, quietly making peace with the sound of your entire dining set shattering.
3. Drive to your new apartment unaided by rearview mirrors or windows (which are blocked by your life now stuffed in boxes), using only prayer to protect you every time you change lanes.
4. Haul the boxes up four flights of stairs, causing enough damage to floors and doorways that you can say with absolute certainty that you've already forfeited your security deposit.

5. Repeat this sixteen more times because your smart car only fits three boxes at a time. But you're moving two people. That should make things easier, right? Two bodies, two sets of hands? Sure, but also: twice as much stuff. All of the above still applies, except now you have to budget time for arguing. Take the previous list, and add the following:

1a. Fight about what you should keep and what you should throw out. Do this until you hear yourself saying something like, "OK, but when the Jets win the Super Bowl and I don't have every jersey a family member has gotten me for the past twelve Christmases, that's gonna be on *you!*"

2a. Argue about whether it's more feminist to help carry boxes or compensate the wage gap by letting your boyfriend do all the work. If you are in a same-sex relationship, skip this step and argue about whose clicky elbow from high school lacrosse is worse.

3a. Help the driver with limited visibility navigate by screaming, "Holy shit, you almost got us killed!" every time you change lanes.

4a. Argue that if you can't handle moving a bunch of boxes, how are you going to handle having kids or a parent dying? Cry.

5a. Repeat steps 1–5, each time more upset.

This is also a great chance to test your friendships. After your partner storms off, you'll need to hit up your friends to help move the rest of the stuff that's still sitting on the sidewalk. Like now, if they don't mind. It's starting to rain. Is a PlayStation 4 waterproof?

Hooray! The two of you have made the crotch-splitting leap to cohabitation. This is an exciting time when you are both metaphorically and literally building a life together (i.e., you're building trust but also an IKEA Ramsätra TV unit). All the "mines" are now "ours." And if you're like us, that means you now own two pieces of Tupperware, a rusty frying pan, a beach chair, and three and a half copies of *Brave New World*. What a bounty! But it goes without saying that all that plunder does not a Viking's castle make.

When you live with a roommate, no one thinks it's weird if you sleep on a mattress you laid across an old futon frame under a "comforter" of stapled-together complimentary airplane blankets. When you live with a significant other, however, that's not gonna fly. You're not just coexisting in a food and sleep pod. You're building a home together. And your home is a reflection of you as a couple.

Unfortunately, just because you're adult enough to make a decision like this, doesn't mean you're adult enough to know what the hell a wall sconce is.

HOW TO DECORATE LIKE THE ADULTS YOU AREN'T

There are a lot of styles out there. Mid-Century Modern. Alpine Rustic. Shabby Chic. Put two words together and they're probably a school of interior design. Retro Grunge. Ass Sandwich. OK, maybe not. Let's cut to the chase and tell you what you really need to know to look like an adult couple, even though you're still surprised you have to do taxes every year.

- **Succulents.** You gotta get some fucking succulents. First off, they're resilient and don't need to be watered. Even better, they already look plastic, so when you buy plastic ones, they still look real.

- **Pictures.** Now that you're dating, you have to display pictures of yourselves dating. No clue why. It seems a little desperate, like, "Of course we didn't marry for the green card, look at all these pictures of us hugging in different locations!" Make sure to put these desperate pictures in equally desperate frames that have **LOVE** or **JOY** written on them, in case your guests can't read the emotion in your vacant smiles.

- **Art.** This one's hard, because art is so subjective. It can be a photograph of a bike in black and white, a painting of wine next to some grapes, or a vintage Guinness ad. Literally any of those three things.

- **Candles.** These are like succulents in that you're supposed to clutter them on every unoccupied surface in your apartment. The more the scent sounds like the name of a strip club, the better: Midnight Oasis, Candy Cane Lane, Cinnamon Scone, ✖✖✖ Fully Nude Girls Exposed, etc.

- **Books.** Not every book is fit to be displayed. For example, no one needs to know you're *Journaling Your Way to a Sexier You* or *Eliminating Gluten to Find God*. However, everyone *does* need to know that you read Kurt Vonnegut and David Foster Wallace. A good bookshelf should appear highbrow while actually just trying to appeal to the widest possible audience. Like a porn star who wears glasses!

- **Bookends.** Try to find some African animal ones. African animals made out of wood are adult as fuck.

- **Instruments.** Do you play guitar? Give off a creative vibe by mounting it on your wall! Not a guitar player? Even better! Just mount it a little higher so the instrument is conveniently out of reach whenever one of your friends asks you to jam.

- **Accent Wall.** Wanna paint your walls but don't wanna paint your walls? Find the tiniest "wall" in your apartment and paint that! It definitely makes a statement! Namely, "We tried!"

- **Free-Floating Shelves That Are Just There to Hold Trinkets.** A free-floating shelf is the perfect home for snow globes, fake fruit, and wooden block letters that spell out FAMILY. Why do you have these things in the first place? Because adults give each other terrible gifts and it's considered impolite to put them in the garbage.

- **A Bar Cart.** Not only are alcohol bottles and cocktail supplies useful for when you want to drink, they add a classy, *Mad Men* touch that, for some reason, no one ever associates with lite alcoholism.

- **A Wine Rack.** See "Bar Cart." Somehow, you're allowed to have both and you're STILL not a raging alcoholic!

- **Empty Jack Daniel's Bottles Everywhere.** Ditto. This just screams fun couple!

There! You're on your way to successfully impersonating a *real adult relationship*. But all those succulents and empty Jack Daniel's bottles won't be fooling anyone if they're covered in a layer of dust mites and bacon grease. That kind of class requires maintenance.

If you're like us, the beginning of your cohabitation will be a perpetual state of ping-ponging responsibility. But having a significant other who cooks and cleans up after you isn't a healthy partnership. If you don't share the burdens of daily life, you could wind up resenting each other. That's why it's important to . . .

DISTRIBUTE THE CHORES SO YOU'RE EQUALLY NOT DOING THEM

Did you know that people are disgusting? It's true. Each one comes with their very own trail of filth. So while you're happy to inherit their round-the-clock companionship and wide-screen TV, you're also inheriting their dirty dishes, sweaty workout clothes, and enough pubic hair to clog the Siberian sinkhole. These "totems of humanity" will summon a blazing, white-hot ire in you, until you realize—if they're disgusting, that means you get a free pass to be disgusting too.

As you begin to share the responsibility of avoiding responsibility, it's important to make sure you are *equally* half-assing it. Otherwise *resentment* could grow in your relationship, much like that invasive mold in your shower, which may or may not be responsible for the raspy cough and mild back acne you have now. It's not sexy, but a chore chart can be a relationship-saver. It takes all the guessing out of "Am I cleaning more than my partner?" and confirms that neither of you is doing anything.

HALF-ASSED CHORE CHART

	EMILY	MURPH
MONDAY	Flip couch cushions to hide weird stains.	Smoosh surface crumbs into hidden depths of shag rug.
TUESDAY	Tie trash bag to contain the garbage stink.	Add water to the remnants of the same bottle of hand soap we've had our entire relationship.
WEDNESDAY	Put things that are on counters and tables in closets and drawers instead.	Open a window and hope the flies fly out.
THURSDAY	Run butt wipes over sticky surfaces.	Throw out Tupperware so we never have to know what it smelled like in there.
FRIDAY	Buy black towels so no one will notice when they get dirty.	Throw out any clothing labeled "hand wash only" and replace with denim 'cause that shit doesn't need to be washed.
SATURDAY	Run shower to clean it because it cleans itself, it's water.	Light scented candles near that water stain that seems to be growing.
SUNDAY	Arrange the sea of unnecessary clutter into artful piles of unnecessary clutter.	Get takeout so we don't have to do dishes.

Once you've systematically neglected all cleanliness protocol and slapped your stink over every square inch of your new apartment, it's gonna be hard to leave that puppy! Now comes the hermit phase of your cohabitation—when the excitement and novelty of your new living situation meets your growing codependence. You won't be leaving the house for a while, so order some takeout, and get that wide-screen hummin'—you're ready to consume some sensationalist media about other people's misfortunes!

WHICH STREAMING SERVICE HAS THE BEST MURDER PORN?

Since you don't plan on leaving the house anytime soon, you're going to want to invest in the right streaming service. While you'd like to imagine yourself viewing Emmy-award-winning series and critically acclaimed art films, let's be real—you're going to watch true crime docu-series about guys who maybe/probably killed some lady. Why? Because you're in a loving, committed relationship, which means you don't have to pretend to be anything other than a trashy monster. You can't afford to subscribe to every service, so let's run through each one's murder porn library and find one that caters to your twisted sensibilities.

- **Netflix.** Why Netflix and chill when you can Netflix and KILL? The streaming service also boasts the largest collection of murder porn, including documentaries about H. H. Holmes (a man with his own murder *castle*) and a monster named Cropsey who may or may not live in the woods of Long Island (fingers crossed). It also features original, exclusive murder porn like *Making a Murderer*—a show so good, it made the world believe that a dude who once threw a cat in a fire was innocent. Netflix also provides a slew of fake murder porn like *The Fall*, *Broadchurch*, *The Killing*, *Twin Peaks*, and a billion other knockoffs, so even the biggest loser couple should be entertained for at least a weekend!

- **Amazon.** Of the popular streaming apps, Amazon offers the least free murder porn. However, it does allow you to buy or rent your murder porn à la carte. And, if you know how to work the system, you can use the app to download free trials of *other apps* to watch rare murder porn that isn't carried by other streaming services. Download a free trial of Sundance Now (who actually pays for this shit?) and watch *The Staircase*—a docu-series about a dude who had not one but two women fall down the stairs and die while alone with him. It's a fascinating true crime whodunit! Even though heprobablydunit.

- **HBO.** HBO features *The Jinx*, the only murder porn docu-series that actually solves the goddamn murder instead of leaving you hanging (we're looking at you, *Serial*). Additionally, of all the Kurt Cobain documentaries—it's a rule that every third documentary needs to be about Kurt Cobain—HBO's *Montage of Heck* is probably the best. At the very least, the fact that it's mostly home videos makes it the most invasive, and we know you love that, you sick piece of shit. HBO also has the fantastic fake murder porn series *True Detective*. Unfortunately, it also has *True Detective* Season 2.

- **Hulu.** Hulu quietly boasts one of the best selections of murder porn out there. You'll need to comb through their catalog of kids' shows and *The Bachelor* spin-offs to find its seedy underbelly, but once you do? Oh baby.

  Hulu streams shows from Investigation Discovery, a cable channel that is essentially 24/7 murder porn. Specifically murder porn that is entirely trashy reenactments and doesn't even try to fool you with artsy documentary footage filmed from inside a moving car. You can stream primo death-smut like *Scorned: Love Kills, Southern Fried Homicide,* and *Psychic Investigators*. If you like terrible acting and watching people kill each other in lingerie—look no further. Our favorite is *Swamp Murders.* You'd think that they'd eventually run out of murders that took place in swamps, but nope!

...

Maybe it's your murder porn–fueled fear of the outside world, or maybe it's a general codependent sloth, but moving in together will sharply increase your likelihood to bail on social engagements. But what about big events that you feel obligated to attend? What if, heaven forbid, you're invited to a friend's birthday?

SHOULD YOU GO TO YOUR FRIEND'S BIRTHDAY AT A BAR?
A QUIZ

Bears hibernate. Humans cancel plans and order Thai Palace Fun Yum. Being in love is an amazing opportunity to live up to your idealized reflection in the eyes of someone you admire. It's also a great excuse to ditch everything you've ever committed to. If your relationship is going well, you will have successfully ghosted every friendship you've had for the past twenty-seven years in favor of this person you've, comparatively, just met.

This kind of behavior is totally acceptable in the winter. I mean, the weather is frightful! What choice do you have other than RSVP-ing to something you know you're not going to attend then canceling via text two hours before? But by spring, you're expected to emerge from your hermit hole and show off your Netflix-induced jaundice. Deciding whether or not you can bail on an event, like, say, your *Friend's Birthday at a Bar* becomes less obvious. Let this quiz decide for you!

1. *How close are you with this person?*
    A. Coworkers.
    B. Acquaintances.
    C. Friends.
    D. Best friends since the maternity ward.

2. *Are you busy tonight?*
    A. Yes, we have some important work we need to get done.
    B. Maybe, we have something earlier that might conflict.
    C. Sorta, there are a few things to do around the house.

D. Technically, no. We've known about this for months.
I helped plan the party.

3. ***Do you have something to do tomorrow that could be affected by a hangover?***
   A. Yes, early in the morning.
   B. Yes, in the afternoon.
   C. Yes, at night.
   D. No. We've alienated all our friends by bailing on them and this is the last person who would ever invite us anywhere.

4. ***How far away is this bar?***
   A. Long drive.
   B. Short drive.
   C. Walking distance.
   D. We live in the apartment above it and have one of those poles that firemen use leading directly to it.

5. ***What is the weather like tonight?***
   A. It's raining.
   B. It's supposed to rain later.
   C. It's nice out.
   D. It's so beautiful that artists and photographers are flocking here to capture the night's majesty.

6. ***How expensive is this place?***
   A. Very pricey.
   B. Middle of the road.
   C. Cheap.

D. Free. Top shelf open bar and they're giving out goodie bags with expensive electronics so we stand to make money.

7. *Who else is going?*
    A. Nobody we know.
    B. A few people we know.
    C. A lot of people we know.
    D. Everyone we know, including family who flew in from abroad.

8. *Did this person come to your birthday at a bar?*
    A. No.
    B. Yes, but only for a little bit.
    C. Yes, they were there the whole time.
    D. No. It hasn't happened yet. This party tonight is also my party. It's my joint birthday party with my best friend.

Mostly As—No, you don't have to go. A coworker isn't worth a long trip to make awkward conversation in an expensive bar while holding an umbrella.

Mostly Bs—No, you don't have to go. A mere acquaintance is not worth shelling out medium bucks on a mildly unpleasant night!

Mostly Cs—No, you don't have to go. *Sure*, this person is a good friend. *Yes*, the bar sounds pretty cool. And, *fine*, it is within walking distance. *But* you already took your pants off. Send them a text tomorrow about how fun the party was and hope they drank so much that they won't remember that you didn't show.

Mostly Ds—UGH! Yes, you do have to go. There's no excuse for missing your lifelong best friend's birthday party, in the bar that you designed, that's connected to your apartment, that your family considered important enough to cross the world for, that happens to also be your birthday party. Put on a brave face and try your best to have fun![11]

Cohabitation is bliss! At least until the day, a few months in, when the two of you wake up, look in the mirror and behold the sad losers staring back at you, ten pounds heavier with a dangerous vitamin D deficiency. When that happens, it's time to emerge from your cocoon of crusty blankets and become beautiful social butterflies.

REPAIR THE FRIENDSHIPS YOU DESTROYED WHILE YOU WERE FALLING IN LOVE

You steered every topic of conversation to your new relationship, then became a condescending love guru, and finally, you flat out ignored them. Considering that we told you to do most of those things, we will accept partial blame. But, in our humbly infallible opinion, you needed that alone time to grow as a couple. Besides, it's easy to win friends back. At least, it's easier than trying to make new ones, since making friends as an adult is like begging strangers to spend time with you. Oh wait, that's exactly what it is.

---

11   Nurse one drink, only talk to each other, then leave by 9 P.M.

When making amends, don't apologize. Apologizing is admitting fault, and you're not looking to grow as a person. You just want people to hang out with in case you run out of murder porn. If you follow our advice, you can seamlessly reenter your friend group without anyone acknowledging that you were ever AWOL. That is your goal here—not forgiveness, but *forget-ness.*

Send an email about a group get-together: "We haven't seen you guys in so long! We've been so busy!" Since all group email invites end with either zero replies or a long, confusing thread of inside jokes, this email is less an attempt to hang out and more a reminder of your existence. You are ready to be friends again! On your schedule, of course.

Follow up with a group text. This will allow you to infiltrate their phones. You see, every friend group has a go-to text chain that they use to make plans and share screen caps of crazy Facebook statuses from people they went to high school with. Problem is, you've been gone so long, your friends have probably started a new one without you. The solution? Establish your text thread as the preferred one by constantly pushing it to the top of their inbox. Load up on screen caps and inside jokes. Take the focus off of your absence by making fun of Jared Spheen from pre-calc's three paragraph rant about secular holiday cups at Starbucks.

As soon as you're back in their phones, you're privy to all casual group hangs. If someone's watching the Packers at a bar or having people over to meet their dog, they'll text it to the group, making you, by default, invited. You're free to just start showing up to shit as if nothing happened! And once you're around enough, they'll have no choice but to take you back. Confronting you would take way too much energy, and adults don't have energy!

Oh, but study up. Make sure you're informed on all the group drama. You don't want to wonder aloud when Keenan and Lindsey are going to get engaged only to find out that Keenan and Lindsey broke up on the cruise that everyone went on without you. Then you won't get invited on next year's cruise!

After a few weeks of showing up unannounced, you may even feel bold enough to invite people to your place. Hosting a dinner party allows you to have the best of both worlds—being social without having to leave the house.

Unfortunately, this means you'll need to buy wine.

HOSTING A DINNER PARTY WHEN YOU DON'T KNOW SHIT ABOUT WINE

Nothing screams, "We are an adult couple and you have to respect our relationship," like offering your guests a bottle of wine. But what if you don't know a Pinot Noir from a Pinot Grigio, a Merlot from a Malbec, or a Bordeaux from a butthole? Not to worry, we'll answer all your questions with the crisp clarity of a young Riesling.

What type of wine should I get? Get red wine. White wine is universally looked down upon, unless Drake's[12] gonna be there, in which case you might wanna grab some, and perhaps a rosé.[13] But the average person who pretends to like wine prefers the "full-bodied" and "earthy" reds.

---

12 *Good weed, white wine/I come alive in the nighttime*—"What's My Name," Rihanna, feat. Drake
13 *Cups of the rosé/Bitches in my old phone*—"Marvin's Room," Drake

How much should I spend on it? Wine pricing can be pretty arbitrary and focus group after focus group has found that price doesn't necessarily correlate with taste. At the same time, you don't want your guests to mistake you for a *skimp*anzee.[14] That's why we recommend you buy one expensive bottle and leave the price tag on. Everyone will see this and assume the rest of your Chateau Cheap Ass is similarly priced. Save even more money by stealing the price tag off of an expensive bottle of wine and never buying it in the first place!

Do I have to talk about it? Yes! If you don't, your ignorance will be assumed. Ignorant until proven pretentious!

What should I say about it? Say things like *earthy, mossy, robust, toasty, structured.* Think of a wet lawn first thing in the morning and compare your wine to stuff you might find on it. *Grassy and mineral-ly. Oaky with a hint of charcoal. A wet tennis ball. Dew-speckled skateboard.* Compare it to fruits that aren't grapes. We know, confusing, considering it is filled with grapes and will most likely taste like grapes. But don't say grapes. Say *huckleberry jam with a touch of lingonberry.*

Will I sound like an asshole when I talk about wine? We hope so. If you get through your description of that '15 Merlot that cost $52.00[15] and you're *not* thinking of donating to NPR to try to win tickets to the summer stock ballet, then you're not doing it right.

---

14 Frugal ape.
15 $4.99.

What should I "pair" it with? If there's one thing everyone agrees is good with wine, it's cheese. Spend most of your dinner budget on cheese wheels, unnecessarily fancy crackers, and a hunk of chalkboard to serve them on because, who knows, that's just something people do. If you have a little extra, get some tiny knives that you can't use on anything else. Ya know, *cheese knives*. Sure, this seems like a lot, but the rest of your dinner is gonna be pasta and bread rolls, and that shit is like war-rations cheap.

Does this mean I have to bring wine when I go to *other* people's dinner parties? Unfortunately, yes. Most of being an adult is bringing wine someone else brought to your house to someone else's house. Within any friend group, the same three bottles of wine are circulating, and will continue to do so for an average of five years before someone finally drinks them. When you host a dinner party, you're essentially building an arsenal of wines to bring to other people's dinner parties.

Why are we doing this? Because it allows us to perpetuate the binge-drinking of our youth, without the stigma associated with twenty- and thirty-somethings getting drunk on a Tuesday night. We drink as much as we did in college, but we also *eat*. We're matching alcohol to food, pound for pound, baby. And that's *responsible*.

I still don't *know* anything about wine. Neither does anybody else!

Well done. That was adult as fuck. And it only gets adultier from here. Since you've been living together, it's likely that you've floated around the idea of getting engaged. But before you make any big decisions, it's imperative that you get on the same page about the future. And that means talking about kids.

ARE YOU PLANNING ON HAVING FRIENDS WITH KIDS?

Having friends with kids is a huge responsibility. It's not for everyone. Maybe you like swearing and having a child in the room would cut into that. Maybe you have ambitions outside of liking Facebook pictures of wispy-haired toddlers in pumpkin patches. Maybe you're terrified your friends will ask you to hold the baby and you won't know what to do with the head because its neck doesn't work yet and you're afraid you'll kill it.

Many couples choose not to have friends with kids and find fulfilling friendships with like-minded couples who also value disposable income over propagating the human race. Before you decide if having friends with kids is right for you, it's important to ask yourselves a few questions.

- **Are you prepared for the personal sacrifice?** Once you have friends with kids, life is no longer about you. It's about your friends' kids. A nonexistent sleep schedule, finicky eating habits, temper tantrums—just a few of the many things that your friends won't shut up about. If having kids is a full-time job, then having friends with kids is a part-time job where you listen to your friends talk about how having kids is a full-time job. Sow your oats now, because soon your conversations will revolve around things like whether or not the baby likes oats.

- **On that note, have you talked to your partner about who will be primarily responsible for talking about their kids?** With the rise of progressive hashtags like #dadswithbabies, men are pretending to care about children more than ever. Still, the brunt of baby talk usually falls on the woman. Before you commit to friends with kids, decide: Will you have a traditional relationship where the woman talks to the mom about the baby while the man talks to the dad about work? Or will you take a more balanced approach, where you're both talking about the baby while constantly checking your phone to see if you can leave yet?

- **Are you OK with staying in on a Saturday night?** When your friends have kids, they need to be at home to make sure their kids don't die. If they go out with you, they need to hire someone else to make sure their kids don't die. That requires planning. Gone are the days when you could just text your friends for a spontaneous night out. Fun is now rigorously regimented. Fun must be planned weeks ahead. Fun ends at ten because they "miss the baby," or as you like to tell them after nine beers, they "forgot how to party."

- **How will you discipline your friends with kids?** Friends with kids frequently bail on plans and need to be called out. Will you roast them via group text? Make fun of them behind their backs with other childless couples? Tell them to their faces that this little parasite is ruining your friendship? It's important to present a unified front when throwing shade.

- **Have you considered what religion your friends will be raising their kids?** Christian kids mean a christening and a baptism and a communion. That's a lot of weekend time. A Jewish kid requires less commitment up top, but eventually, you're gonna have to write a fat bat mitzvah check. You may want to stick to the little heathens raised by your "spiritual, but not religious" friends. You won't have to go to church, but you'll still get leftover Christmas cookies.

- **Will you have one set of friends with kids, or more?** As a childless couple, you can't fully relate to your friends with kids, so you'll never be able to fulfill all their social needs. As they always remind you, "You'll never understand until you have kids of your own." You may end up deciding that the healthiest thing is to have multiple sets of friends with kids so they can keep each other entertained. The only downside is that you'll have even more people in your life saying, "You'll never understand until you have kids of your own."

- **Are you having friends with kids to save your own relationship?** You might be tempted to take on friends with kids to make your own relationship look better by comparison. "Sure, we fight all the time, but at least we don't have to watch *Frozen* twice a day!" Let's be clear: friends with kids will not fill the hole in your relationship. You will have all the same problems and you'll have to go to a four-year-old's birthday party on a Saturday. That's kids, new parents, and clowns on a Saturday.

    All in all, having friends with kids might seem like more trouble than it's worth—but it can also be a very rewarding experience. Years down the line, when one of your friends' kids looks up at you and affectionately calls you "Aunt" or "Uncle," you'll realize that it was all worth it.

Plus, when they're older, they can help you move!

If you're ready to brave the horror that is hanging out with new parents, you're ready to brave anything. You have our blessing, you crazy kids! POP. THAT. QUESTION!

GETTING
ENGAGED

—Our Story—

We got engaged in Costa Rica 'neath a
lullaby of screaming howler monkeys.
The next day, one of the monkeys threw
poop in the pool.

VI.

If you like attention, you're going to *love* getting engaged. You're constantly being congratulated on something you haven't even done yet. All you do is buy a ring and post pictures of yourselves, then everyone in your life says how happy they are for you. You can even hire a photographer to take more pictures of you, then mail those pictures to people, and it isn't weird like it should be.

Engagement is the brief window when people are willing to celebrate your love without expecting a meal and three hours of a DJ in exchange. Milk it for all it's worth. After this, you'll have to plan a wedding, and the greedy claws of the commercial wedding industry will bleed you dry.

Speaking of blood, let's pick out your engagement ring!

PICK THE PERFECT BLOOD DIAMOND
FOR YOUR ENGAGEMENT RING

So, the two of you are ready to make a lifelong commitment, and you've decided to forgo a blood oath ritual in favor of an engagement ring. Don't worry, you'll still have *plenty* of blood on your hands! A diamond ring is the perfect way to symbolize your eternal love for each other and your eternal indifference to the complicated politics of diamond trafficking. Let's go shopping!

Other precious stones are surging in popularity, but like the ruthless despots of West Africa, the diamond is still king. Despite easy access to highly detailed information,[16] the majority of couples *still* choose diamond engagement rings. It could be that they're more traditional. It could be that they hate Zimbabwe. Either way, there are a lot of things to think about before buying a luxury item that's caused immeasurable strife. Mainly, how you can get the prettiest diamond for the best price!

When diamond shopping, you should familiarize yourself with the Four Cs—Clarity, Cut, Color, and Carat—while definitely not familiarizing yourself with the egregious human rights violations taking place in Angolan diamond mines. Now, you probably have a few questions. Namely, "What do the Four Cs mean?" and, "What is an Angolan diamond mine?" We'll answer the first part!

Clarity refers to the number and size of the diamond's imperfections. For example, a diamond with no imperfections is considered *flawless*, whereas the idea of "conflict free" diamonds is extremely *flawed* because it only accounts for diamonds illegally sold by rebel armies and not corrupt governments who mistreat their own people. Some diamonds appear flawless to the naked eye, but have minor imperfections under magnification. This is an excellent way to save money on

---

16 See *Blood Diamond* starring Leonardo DiCaprio.

a ring! If it looks good, why look any deeper? Why look beyond the surface of this beautiful diamond and learn the horrifying truth?

Cut, not to be confused with the financial cut that smugglers get by circumventing diamond trade agreements and selling internationally, refers to the diamond's sparkle. This "sparkle" is the most subjective aspect of the diamond and is difficult to analyze. But just because something is difficult doesn't mean we should ignore it, right? At least, not when it comes to diamond prettiness! Cuts are ranked from "Poor" to "Excellent," and if you're buying a diamond, you certainly don't want to waste your time worrying about anything that is poor!

Next is **Color**. The less color in the stone, the more valuable it is. Funny how diamonds mimic so much of society! A diamond with a D rating is completely clear and considered perfect. Interestingly enough, there are no A, B, or C ratings. It's almost like, no matter how good of a diamond you get, you're still failing the people of Liberia!

Finally, **Carat** refers to the size of the diamond. Large stones are very rare, so price increases exponentially with size. At the same time, flaws in the diamond will become more obvious, so bigger isn't necessarily better. Just ask the rebel armies of Sierra Leone, who are more than happy to force small children to fight in their diamond wars!

Now that you know your Four Cs, how do you apply them to diamond buying? Obviously, you can't buy a perfect diamond. They're incredibly rare and expensive. Plus, it would be strange to call anything perfect that puts weapons in the hands of African warlords. Your priorities when buying a diamond should look something like this:

- *Cut*
- *Color*
- *Clarity*
- *Carat*
- *Human Lives*

We know, *we know*: this list is bound to spark some controversy. You might be one of those people who values *clarity* more than *color*. Either way, both sides can agree that a diamond's overall appearance is far more important than its size or the well-being of people in Third World countries.

The only thing left now is to pick a shape. For you? We'd suggest a heart![17]

...

To anyone who's planning on proposing: you've got a lot on your plate. Not only must you actually *grovel*—begging someone who is supposed to be your equal while they *literally* look down on you—but, in some cases, you'll also have to beg her dad.

---

17 You monster.

HOW TO ASK FOR HER DAD'S PERMISSION
LIKE A GOOD LITTLE BOY

You can't trust your girlfriend to make a decision for herself. Yes, she has her own apartment and pays her own bills, but when it comes down to making big decisions like who to bone, her father knows best. It's a longstanding tradition to ask for the father's blessing, harkening back to the days when women were just part of a dowry transaction. It's like trading livestock. Would you just run onto a farm and start having sex with one of the sheep? No, you'd check with the farmer first!

Asking her dad can be intimidating. The type of man who expects this formality is probably pretty traditional. And traditional guys tend to own guns. But since you and your girlfriend are hapless toddlers who can't make a life decision without parental approval, you're going to need to confront this grizzly bear of a human before you can proceed.

Take a deep breath. This will be tough, but it's important. Nobody understands what it's like to be a young woman like a fifty-five-year-old man.

STEP ONE

Set the tone with a manly one-on-one. Take him to a *man* place. A cigar bar within a strip club should do nicely. If there are any women around, kindly ask them to leave. Better yet, in the spirit of the occasion, kindly ask *their fathers* to *tell them* to leave. Show up early and pick two seats at the bar. Saw off the bottom of his stool so that it's shorter and he has to look up at you. Wear something that makes you look intimidating, like a shark tooth necklace or a 1980s businesswoman suit with shoulder pads.

STEP TWO

When he arrives, be straightforward. This is a no-nonsense guy who doesn't tolerate nonsense guys who say nonsense stuff. Prove that you are his equal. Look him straight in the eye and say, "Sir, I would like to marry your daughter, and since I am a cowardice toad, I won't do it unless you are OK with it, sir. Please, sir."

Herein lies the catch-22 of asking a manly man if you can marry his daughter. A manly man wants his daughter to marry a real guy's guy who respects tradition, but a real guy's guy does what he damn well pleases and doesn't need to ask permission. So what do you do if *respecting tradition* means *asking permission*? Wow, all this testosterone is making us dizzy!

STEP THREE

Haggle. Promise to name your firstborn son after him. Dudes love it when you name sons after them. You can even offer a caveat that you'll change the kid's name if he grows up to be a wiener. Like one of those little shits who puts on headphones at the table on Thanksgiving. Assure him that, in the unlikely event that his namesake disgraces him, you'll start calling him Travis.

STEP FOUR

Disclose your tax returns. Your proof of earnings should demonstrate your ability as a breadwinner, without emasculating him. You can just forge these documents, since his wife does all the paperwork and it's likely he's never seen them. They should include charitable donations, but only to local religious organizations. That way, you'll make it clear that you are a good person insofar as you care about your family and neighborhood, but could honestly give a shit about the rest of the country. Like every Good American Man.

STEP FIVE

Seal the deal with a firm handshake. Your grip should be strong enough to maim, but not kill, a large woodland creature. This demonstrates that you are both powerful and respectful, like a big dog who knows his place. Maintain eye contact for at least five solid shakes, then raise a toast with a non-light beer. Congratulations, you've bagged yourself a father-in-law! Welcome to the family![18]

Aren't proposals strange? You arrive at the conclusion of marriage *together*. You go ring shopping and pick one out *together*, using the *shared budget* you came up with based on *both of* your *jobs*. Then, at the last minute, you abandon it all and make the man pretend like it was his idea all along! So how do you blindside someone who not only knows you're coming, but actually helped you get there?

---

18 A family you could lose in a divorce.

HOW TO *SURPRISE* HER, EVEN THOUGH
YOU JUST PICKED OUT A RING TOGETHER

This isn't going to be easy. You've got to do the proposal equivalent of faking your own death, throwing a smoke bomb, then showing up in their bedroom armoire two days later with a katana to their throat. You must become an *engagement ninja*, which is why we've turned to Sun Tzu's *Art of War*.

"Hide order beneath the cloak of disorder . . ."
You must project the illusion of uncertainty. Talk about traveling, but without her. Start following porn stars on Twitter. Meet up with an ex "for work." She'll be so busy worrying that you're going to leave her, it'll come completely out of left field when you put down the suitcase you packed to leave her and pull out that gorgeous rock. Also, not a bad idea to literally wear a cloak.

"The natural formation of the country is the soldier's best ally."
Learn her emotional terrain. Find her "mountains" of insecurity and "rivers" of jealousy. Set psychological mines like, "I can't believe your friend Emma is still single!" and "Your sister looks great in blue," then wait for them to explode!

"O divine art of secrecy! Through you we learn to be invisible!"
True love is built on trust, but engagement is built on secrets. *Especially* when it comes to the ring. Once it's in your possession, you must do everything short of a presidential motorcade to protect it. Put it in a condom and swallow it, then poop it out at a romantic moment. Have

it surgically implanted. Bake it into a loaf of pumpernickel bread that she won't go near cuz she's "gluten-sensitive."

"Those who are skilled in producing surprises will win."
Romantic dinners and Caribbean vacations are all too obvious. She is gonna be stop-and-frisking you every day, trying to find that box-shaped bulge in your khakis. The most surprising thing you can do at a candlelit dinner on your last night in Turks and Caicos is *not* propose.

"In the midst of chaos, there is also opportunity."
Fire drills, crowded bars, funerals . . . *these* are your chances to catch her off guard.

"Let your plans be dark and impenetrable as the night . . ."
Keep her guessing. "Where are we going?" Don't tell her. "Do I have to wear this blindfold?" Don't answer. "Who are you?" Again, nothing, unless you have a voice modulator.

"Take advantage of the enemy's unreadiness, make your way by unexpected routes, and attack unguarded spots. . . . Perfect timing allows an eagle to pounce on its prey for the kill."
Propose while she is taking a shit.

But what if you don't want to propose in an intimate, quiet space like the crapper? What about the attention whores?

HOW TO RUIN YOUR PROPOSAL BY
TRYING TO MAKE IT GO VIRAL

People have been using their relationships to court undeserved praise for *centuries*. Whether it's an Elizabethan woman flaunting her ostentatious "engagement hat," an ancient Egyptian parading his naked wife in the Festival of Hot Wives, or a modern woman wearing a bride-to-be sash at the Magic Mike show in Vegas, engaged couples feed off attention. Unfortunately, the act of getting engaged is often private and meaningful. So how do you whore out your proposal and turn it into a spectacle?

Propose in public. If you're one of those shrinking violets who thinks, "I'm gonna do it on a bearskin rug in a cabin I rented for New Year's Eve," that cabin better be rigged with cameras, microphones, and all your friends and family waiting to perform a choreographed dance. Think of it as a surprise party meets a Broadway musical meets a YouTube channel that you're trying to get off the ground. If your proposal doesn't lead to a sponsorship deal down the line, then why are you proposing at all?

It's not easy to go viral these days. *Oh, you hired a flash mob?* Everyone hires a flash mob. That's about as obligatory as getting down on one knee. *You flew in her family?* Unless all of them are on active military duty and you're planning on reuniting them with their pets while you propose, you're about as viral as your dad's vacation slideshow. *Your future fiancée is deaf, and you're getting her cochlear implants so the first thing she'll ever hear is "Will you marry me?"* OK, that's pretty good.

In order to rack up the views, you need to get a big reaction from your significant other.[19] Problem is, any normal human is going to be turned off by your obvious attempt at Internet fame. It takes a special kind of person (see: attention monster) to act natural while you shove a camera in their face and profess your love via parody-rap set to the *Fresh Prince of Bel-Air* theme song. But if you've truly found The One, they should share your values. Specifically, your deep desire to have a satellite interview with *Good Morning America*.

Some people will tell you that a shameless attention grab is a bad way to start your life together. But those nobodies will go their whole lives without ever being featured on BuzzFeed. You two will have a wonderful future together, full of way-too-personal Facebook statuses and beautiful children who you pimp out to make viral Christmas cards.

Once you've weaseled a "yes" out of your significant other, let the pageantry begin! If a wedding is the Super Bowl, then an engagement is the tailgate. Everybody's so excited for the main event, they can't help but party in the parking lot!

WAYS TO STRETCH YOUR ENGAGEMENT CELEBRATION TO ITS ABSOLUTE LIMIT

The engagement period has become so much more than just an eight- to fourteen-month buffer for your friends to remember to RSVP to your wedding. It's become a celebration *in itself*. A gaggle of mini-

---

19 Preferably a positive one, but you can always reframe it as a prank.

parties to prep you for The Big One. It's like booking a trip to Hawaii, then spending the next six months going to Tiki bars to get excited.

- **Engagement Announcement.** Tell the world! Reaching out to friends individually will only come back to bite you in the ass. Somehow, "Don't say anything before I get a chance to tell everyone," is always heard as, "Smugly insinuate you know something until you accidentally give it away." Since you don't want to risk disrespecting one of your friends, disrespect *all* your friends with a mass, impersonal social media announcement.

  Have fun with it. Don't just post a status that says "I said yes!!" Print it in calligraphy on a chalkboard or a body part (preferably a hand and not, say, a boob). Enroll in flight school, log forty to fifty hours of supervised cockpit experience, and write it across the sky! Or, share a pic of two Starbucks cups labeled "Mr." and "Mrs." This is a great choice for the couple who wants to integrate a corporate powerhouse into their engagement for some reason!

- **Engagement Drinks.** Your friends are going to want to congratulate you in person. Respond to their personal messages with another mass communiqué: an email invite to meet up for casual, but not so casual that you didn't put down a deposit, celebratory drinks.

  This will be a fun, low-key way to regale everyone with the epic tale of your engagement. Assuming, of course, that they haven't already watched it on BuzzFeed's "10 Proposals That Make Us Go Squeeeeeee" listicle. This is also a chance for everyone ask to see the ring. Get those jagged cuticles under control now, because that hand is gonna make the rounds!

- *Engagement Dinner (with Family).* Bring both families together to celebrate and buy you an expensive meal. This is a special occasion. That means appetizers, desserts, and, *oh yeah*, wine by the bottle. Go ahead and get yourselves a red *and* a white for the table. It's that kinda night!

  In addition to footing the bill, your parents will be on their best behavior. Another family just entered the picture and that's going to mean stiff competition for holiday visits. Break bread and enjoy the peace before Thanksgiving turns into a war zone.

- *Engagement Dinner (with Friends).* Your free meals aren't done yet! Hit "reply all" on those casual drinks for a formal follow-up. You owe your friends the opportunity to buy a meal to go with those drinks they already bought you. Make a reservation for twenty-five at a family-style restaurant so you can share food *and* a proper retelling of your engagement story without the distraction of a crowded bar. Anybody who didn't get a chance to congratulate you or see the ring may now do so. Hopefully your jagged cuticles haven't grown back!

- *Engagement Photo Shoot.* There's no better way to make your engagement a bigger deal than it needs to be than by hiring a professional photographer to follow you to the beach. Enough time has passed since your social media announcement that your friends and family are probably itching for another injection of You. What greater gift than having You show up at their doorstep as a magnet? A "Just-Engaged" photo shoot is very important because it's going to be six months to a year before you stand in front of another photographer, in the same positions, but different clothes. And honestly, who can wait that long?

- *Engagement Ring Photo Shoot.* You've got to make sure your star finds her spotlight. What's an opera without its aria-belting prima donna? Nothing. Just a bunch of baritones running around in tights. Book the photographer for a second day so you can capture that sparkly bastion of love incarnate from every angle. Trust us, when you are eighty-five, you are going to want a picture of a ring on a pillow in a cottage.

- *Engagement Party.* This is the money shot in your escalating build-up of formal events. An engagement party is like a baby shower for adults—not to be confused with the bridal shower, another baby shower for adults. Include fun, thematic games like a *ring* toss (eh? eh?), or a race wearing a literal *ball and chain* (oh no, they didn't!)!

    Try a round of "How Well Do You Know the Bride and Groom" bingo. Ask your guests a series of questions about you as a couple and have them guess the answers on a bingo sheet. It's like a pop quiz about your relationship! They should ace it, so long as they paid diligent attention to your proposal story at your engagement dinner and engagement drinks.

- *Engagement Study Group.* In the event that some of your friends scored poorly on "How Well Do You Know the Bride and Groom" bingo, invite them over for a refresher course. Present a detailed PowerPoint and encourage them to make their own flash cards. If they're willing to put the work in, they still stand a chance of being invited to the wedding.

- *Engagement Test.* Your friends will have two hours to complete the Scantron portion of the test and one hour to complete the essay. Bathroom breaks are to be kept to the minimum, and nobody leaves the gym without a faculty chaperone.

With all your engagement festivities underway, your days of slumming it as someone's "boyfriend" or "girlfriend" are over. Now you're someone's *fiancé*. It's like a promotion! But if your title went from "Junior Executive" to "Pretentious Fuckface."

LEARN TO LOVE THE WORD *FIANCÉ*, UGH

Take a moment to say it out loud. *Fiancé*. Give it a real nasal *Ahh-hhN* and a long, drawn-out *sayyyyyyy*. You'll know if you did it right because a little vomit will trickle out of your nose and any plants near you will die.

The word fiancé is one of the worst things you could have on your tongue, aside from, say, a garbage-water-soaked tampon. Though at least with a garbage-water-soaked tampon, you don't sound like a douchebag to everyone you meet. But here's the problem: what else are you going to say? *Partner*? That works—if you're the type of couple who wears matching chiffon robes and owns a sink that looks like a bowl. For everybody else, *fiancé* is actually the best option.

Don't believe us? We've graded it against the competition on the following pages.

☐ *Fiancé*. Makes you sound like a couple of pretentious assholes riding a Vespa to a farmer's market. On the plus side, it rhymes with Beyoncé. **D+**.

☐ **Betrothed**. Somehow *more* pretentious than fiancé. Doesn't rhyme with Beyoncé. **D–**.

☐ *Future Husband or Future Wife*. Feels like something that would be embroidered on His and Hers sweaters for an engagement photo shoot. **D**.

☐ *Future Mate*. Feels like something that would be embroidered on His and Hers sweaters for an engagement photo shoot, but specifically for two bonded animals at the zoo. **D–**.

☐ *Wife to Be or Husband to Be*. Something about the "to be" makes you seem so needy for your wedding day. If you want to be a cool, detached couple who dgaf about the modern wedding industry, the last thing you want to do is appear excited for your wedding. **D–**.

☐ *Companion*. Sounds like you are on a quest together to destroy the One Ring. Also, people call dogs and horses their companions and you don't want to send the wrong message. Namely, that you have sex with your pets. **D**.

☐ *Better Half*. Unclear if you're engaged, already married, or two people sewn together in a sick Nazi experiment. **D–**.

☐ *Other Half*. Like better half, but objectively worse. Why are you marrying this person if they're just some random, *other* half you had lying around? **F.**

☐ *Lover*. Fucking ew. **F−.**

See? When grading on a curve, fiancé is actually an A+. It's a steep curve, but still. Brush up on that French accent, *mon ami*! Because now that you're engaged, people are only going to want to talk to you about the wedding. And you've got to use *some word* to refer that *Special Person You've Chosen as the Last Person You'll Ever Sleep with Hopefully*. Because Aunt Deb looked real uncomfortable when you said, "This is Gabby, my *Special Person I've Chosen as the Last Person I'll Ever Sleep with Hopefully*!"

Unfortunately, for the ladies, fiancée won't be the only crappy name you'll have pushed on you—the patriarchy will expect you to take his last name. But you can tell the patriarchy to suck a FAT ONE! By downplaying it and phrasing it as politely as possible.

HOW TO TELL YOUR IN-LAWS THAT YOU'RE NOT TAKING THEIR LAST NAME WITHOUT SOUNDING LIKE THE DRIPPY TAMPON OF A FEMINIST THEY SUSPECT YOU ARE

It's unavoidable. It's going to come up. Your future in-laws will say "welcome to the family, Mrs. [Their-Last-Name]." They'll wink and tell you that you're going to need to buy new stationery. Monogrammed hand towels will be stitched the moment you announce your engagement. But why would they just assume that you're going to change your last name? What about your cunty personality gave them the impression that you wanted to be a doting wife?

When breaking the news, be careful. You are walking on eggshells here, and since most eggs were born on farms, they tend to be pretty conservative. The most important thing is to not come across as a feminist. Feminism to Baby Boomers is like the Headless Horseman to Sleepy Hollow: everyone's got a story about how it destroyed a friend of a friend, but none of them have ever actually seen it.

Let's look at some sample dialogues to understand how you might accidentally let your feminist flag fly, and what you can do to prevent that from happening.

"I've established a career with my name."

Yikes, why are you talking about your career? Haven't you noticed that they ask their son about his career but ask you about, well, nothing? No one gives a shit about your career, lady! Your only job, as far as they're concerned, is to pump out grandkids.

Tweak: *"I don't know how to change my name on Facebook."*

Your in-laws can definitely sympathize with not understanding technology. Your mother-in-law still hasn't figured out how to enter *her* name correctly, and to this day shares radio station memes as Miller JoAnne. You can even use this as a segue into talking about how technology is ruining the youth of today (neglecting to mention that they watch eight hours of conservative cable news a day, of course).

"I value my family's legacy. I am proud of who I am and where I've come from."

Legacy. Pride. You're on the right track, but without a strong male protagonist, this sounds dangerously like feminism.

Tweak: *"My brother's infertile. He got his testicles caught in a bike chain when he was three. My father's dying wish was that I would shoulder the burden of carrying on our family name. It is with heavy heart that I must obey his final wish. But don't worry, we're going to hyphenate."*

Legacy. Pride. The need to soothe a male ego. A graphic tale of ruined testicles. Perfect.

"I would like my child to have my name, because I am as much a part of it."

Again, you're talking too much. You just ruined the sweet notion of grandchildren with your liberal salt.

Tweak: *"I want kiiiiiiiids!!!"*

Just say this. The name thing won't even come up. If they ever ask about it, just bring up how much you want kids and hijack every conversation with baby talk. By the time your theoretical future children are born, they'll be so busy criticizing your parenting they won't even notice their hyphenated last name.

"Your last name is associated with one of the largest plantations in the antebellum South."

Again, anything political from the mouth of a woman will automatically be received as an attack. And you don't want to rattle the delicate sensibilities of racists by calling them racists.

Tweak: *"I want kiiiiiiiiiiiiiiiiiiiiiiiiiiiiiiiiids!!!"*

This one can be used in place of a lot of different ones. Nothing like dangling the grandbaby carrot to steer clear of uncomfortable interactions with your in-laws! Feel free to use it if someone accidentally mentions Planned Parenthood or when your father-in-law says something creepy about a weather girl on TV.

"The idea of a woman changing her last name comes from a time when a wife was considered property."
You might as well kill their dog.

Tweak: *"I'm pregnant."*

Hey, sometimes you gotta up the ante. The good news is, you won't have to lose weight for your wedding!

As you can see, navigating your relationship with your future in-laws is tricky. That's why we recommend you minimize how often you have to do it.

ESTABLISH YOUR FAMILY AS THE CHRISTMAS FAMILY BY TURNING YOUR SIGNIFICANT OTHER AGAINST THEIR OWN PARENTS

Ah, the holidays. That magical time of year when we put our differences aside to celebrate togetherness and give each other digital picture frames. Something about that intoxicating cocktail of cold nights, hot cocoa, and spiced cookies makes you want to scream, "Look! You can *upload* your pictures to it!"

Of all the holiday traditions, perhaps the most beloved is *Getting a Week Off*. During this time, it is expected that you'll *Go Home and See Your Family*. But here's where things get sticky. You *two* may have become *one,* but you still have *two* families. How do you divide your time between *two* sets of people who love and need you? Hash it out with your partner. Listen to each other's needs. Come to an agreement that you should only visit your family.

Relationships take compromise. If you cooked, they do the dishes. If you mowed the lawn, they take out the trash. If you cleaned the bathroom, they admit that their family is less fun to visit!

Here's the deal. Your family is better. You know that. We know that. Your family drinks more, but not in that scary *glimpse into your future alcoholism* way. If you all go out for dinner, your dad pays, even if he makes such a big deal about it that it kind of ruins it. You're not totally on the same page politically, but everybody supports gay marriage, so . . . good enough. What right-minded person skims over that glowing list without jumping out of their chair screaming, "Let's rent a Zipcar and make a weekend of it!"

Unfortunately, it's not always that easy. Your partner might be attached to their family. They may be harboring illusions, no doubt planted in them by the very same jerks who raised them, that their family is better or, at the very least, equal. But if the two of you sit down with open minds and hearts, you'll be able to sidestep all the petty politics and just agree: your mom's food is better.

There are some irrefutable *pros* your family has going for it. You know them already. You don't feel shy around them. You don't have to worry about swearing in front of them. They live near a lot of your friends from high school that you only get to see once a year. Whereas your significant other's family is littered with *cons*. Their mom doesn't know what you like to eat. Their dad likes a different football team than you. Not to mention their sister's blank, lifeless stare that seems to fall exclusively on you, even when you're not talking (seriously, what is up with her?).

After weighing the pros of your family and the cons of your significant other's family, the answer should be obvious. The best thing for *both of you* is spending the holidays at your place. In a perfect world, you and your partner would be on the same page about not wanting to visit their family.

Unfortunately, not every couple has already been through three months of fully-nude-sweat-lodge-couples-counseling like we have. Your partner might be irrationally clinging to the idea that their family isn't the lesser family. If that's the case, you might need to gently point them in the right direction. Everyone holds resentment for their family buried deep down. Help them dig it out!

Now, this is a dark path you're walking down. In order to procure exclusive visitation rights for the holidays, you're going to have to subtly manipulate the ecosystem of their family until one whisper creates an imbalance that causes the whole thing to implode. Are you prepared for such emotional witchcraft? Of course you are.

Try planting seeds like, "Is your dad jealous of you?" and "Was your mom joking when she said that thing about your career?" If they have a sibling, ignite whatever rivalry is there (it's there), preferably using their fickle parents' love as the disputed object. Coach them with an observation that appears neutral but really needles them in the ribcage: "Your mom sure talks about your brother a lot!"

After a little while, you'll start to notice them coming around. "My dad always *has* been cagey about my success" or "I wish my mom would stop talking about my brother's new house." This is a great sign. The seeds of doubt are sprouting into bulbs of worry. Soon, they'll blossom into anger flowers. "I hate the parts of me that remind me of my parents" or "I should kick my brother's ass!" Eventually, those angry petals will be wilted by a wintery indifference: "I have no family." Success!

Probably.

There is always the possibility that, when faced with family drama, your partner will decide to *repair* the relationship rather than discard it. Which means *more* family time. Worst case scenario, they may even have *emotional breakthroughs* and come out of it *closer than ever*. Yikes. Your best move here is to play the long game, agreeing, ostensibly, to split time over the holidays.

The key word is *ostensibly*. When the time comes for their family gathering, act standoffish. Quiet. Maybe a little rude, but nothing overt. A few years of this and their family is bound to feed off of your toxic energy, producing a seething, palpable, mutual dislike. Pair an unspoken animosity with a couple bottles of wine and *BOOM!* Cry-erworks. Your partner will be left with a choice: *You* or *Them*. They'll have to choose you. You have a working penis/vagina that's on-limits.

Whether you've quickly tricked your partner into familial excommunication or spent years deceiving them, your family is officially the one, and only, Christmas family (or Hanukkah family, or Kwanzaa family: manipulating your loved ones is nondenominational!) See? Compromise does work! But in the spirit of the holiday season, it's only fair that you mail their family a gift.

Might we suggest a digital picture frame? You can *upload* pictures to it!

While we're on the subject of shitty gifts, building your wedding registry is just around the corner!

THE WEDDING

-Our Story-

We got married in a venue that looked like
The Shire from Lord of the Rings. All of
the tables were named after Middle-earth
locations. Before you ask, yes, we did make
the people we didn't like sit in Mordor.

VII.

From tiptoeing around your families' sensibilities to carelessly stomping on each other's feelings, there are many dances you'll perform while planning a wedding. The good thing is that the choreography is well trod: if you know the moves, you won't be surprised by a sudden dip or when your partner threatens to call the whole thing off because you can't agree on a table runner thread count. The bad thing is, you will fight about table runners.

We know what you're thinking. "Not us! We are a chill couple who is going to have a totally laid-back wedding. **It's just gonna be like, a party at a bar.**" And to that, we say: ha ha ha ha ha hahahahah ha hah ah a hahaha. Ha HAHA. *[tears fill our eyes as our laughter turns to wheezing and we nearly suffocate from laughter] [we sigh with cathartic bliss] [we glow with Buddha-like enlightenment that's, like, also a little smug] [you feel dumb]*

Ah yes, the ol' "party at a bar" routine. We've seen it many times. In fact, we ourselves once polished and performed it all over New York City! Then our families happened. Go ahead, try floating the idea of not having a wedding around your parents. The *best* response you can hope for is awkward silence and an exchange of judgmental looks. The more likely response is flat-out disownment followed by a public flogging.

A wedding isn't about you, it's about your family. Or rather, it's about paying off the life debt you owe them. They raised you from a pint-sized pants-wetter to an acceptable enough adult that someone would want to share a bank account with you. When you think about it that way, it's not crazy at all that they'd want to celebrate the spoils of their labor. The least you can do is plan a wedding. And to that, we say . . .
UUGGGGGGGGGGGGGGHHHHHHHH.[20]

DAMN IT, NOW YOU HAVE TO PLAN THIS THING
A CHECKLIST

Just because you've made peace with the fact that your party at a bar is now a full-scale wedding, doesn't mean you get to sit back and relax. You have a million tiny decisions ahead of you and indifference is not an option. Don't have an opinion on whether the groomsmen should wear regular or pleated cummerbunds? Too bad! Somebody's gotta make the call, or else those dudes are gonna go 'bundless. You're like a Hollywood producer putting together all of the logistics for a script that you don't even like. And instead of getting paid, you spend money!

☐ **SET A BUDGET**—The average cost of a wedding in the United States is $26,645, so if you'd like to have an *average* wedding, your budget should be somewhere between *down payment on a house* and *yearly salary before taxes*. If you're having second thoughts about spending

---

20 Shit fuck shit fuck shit fuck.

so much money on something that only lasts a day, remember that you'll have pictures that last forever. Sorry, *infuriatingly expensive* pictures that last forever.

☐ **RESERVE VENUE**—Regardless of how *laid-back* your location may be, there's nothing chill about booking a venue. Ceremony on the beach? You've still got to book it like any other venue, but now you've gotta bring your own chairs, PA system, and tent in case it starts raining. Public park? Now you're adding "apply for permit" to your to-do list. Even a barn will have a two-year wait list and a 3K deposit. And that's just for a big empty shed. You've still got to fill that shit with flowers and mason jars!

☐ **BOOK FLORISTS**—You've probably attended a wedding and been like, "Wow! This brewery has so many beautiful flowers all over it! Great venue." Wrong, bitches. The venue has nothing to do with it. That brewery smelled like IPA vom before a well-paid florist decorated it. And by decorate, we of course mean "decorate with *flowers*." The mason jars are a *different* company.

☐ **BOOK CATERERS**—Does your venue come with its own caterers? Or will you hire vendors individually, painstakingly coordinate the whole thing, and blow your money à la carte?

While you may find brief respite in spending money on something that you'll actually enjoy, know this: you'll have so many pictures and dances and cake cuttings and speeches that you'll barely have time to eat at all. Absolutely devastating!

☐ **BOOK AN OFFICIANT**—An officiant can make or break your wedding, so choosing one is an excellent use of your anxiety. You can go the religious route and hire a priest to ruin your ceremony by bringing up Hell too much, or you can confuse your guests with a pagan hippie who makes you sip from something called The Earth Chalice. We elected to have one of our friends officiate. It was easy! All we had to do was fill out paperwork, deliver it to a town hall, have it notarized, and *write the entire goddamn ceremony ourselves*.

☐ **BOOK PHOTOGRAPHER**—Perhaps the greatest charlatan in this den of thieves, the photographer preys on the myth that pictures are the most important part of a wedding (false: it's the booze). They will charge absurd fees to do what all of your guests will be doing for free the entire wedding (taking pictures). In the end, this rogue will send you a $5 flash drive and you'll pick two pictures to print out at CVS.

☐ **BOOK DJ OR BAND**—We know what you're thinking: "Can't I just make a playlist and plug in my phone? I've hosted dozens of parties and everyone's always had a lot of fun!" The answer is: no, you absolute fool. Weddings are not a carefree celebration, they are a strictly coordinated effort to impress people. What if you put on a playlist and one of the songs is slightly louder than the other songs? What if a song skips or, God forbid, an ad plays during the reception? Just imagine the ire of all your critics, i.e., your closest friends and family, as they mentally rank you at the bottom of every wedding they've ever been to. Sorry, you're at the very least going to have to hire a DJ. And, if you don't directly tell them not to, they *will* play "Celebration."

☐ **BUY DRESS**—Ladies, it's time for you to invest in the worst cost-to-use purchase you'll make in your entire life: a giant, expensive, unwieldy monstrosity that will only be worn once and possibly not even for the whole day. When you put it on, you'll get to feel like a princess, but only in the way that you can't pee without an attendant.

☐ **REGISTER FOR GIFTS**—This seems like it would be fun, right? You put a big list of things that you want on the Internet and your friends and family buy those things for you. But, much like everything else that *seems* fun about wedding planning, there is a catch. A registry isn't for things you *want*. It's for things *old people think you want*. They assume that you just moved into a giant house together—like they did when they got married—and now you need plates, silverware, and various kitchen gadgets to fill it up. They don't realize that you live in a four-hundred-square-foot apartment with no room for maple syrup cruets, asparagus steamers, or hope for the economy to ever recover.

☐ **RESERVE HOTEL ROOMS**—Because your guests cannot be trusted to book a hotel for themselves.

☐ **RESERVE SHUTTLES**—Because your guests cannot be trusted to not drive drunk.

☐ **MAKE A WEDDING WEBSITE**—This is where you'll post directions to your venue because your guests cannot be trusted to use Google. Also, the date and time of your wedding, because your guests aren't going to read the invitation. Also, a link to your registry, because your guests can't buy a gift without you holding their hand. Also, you can just call the whole thing off and elope, it's not too late.

☐ **PICK OUT BRIDESMAID DRESSES/GROOMSMEN SUITS**—All you need to do here is pick out a bridesmaid dress that flatters the bodies of your model-thin nineteen-year-old cousin and your pregnant sister who is about to enter her third trimester. Don't worry, if you do a bad job, they will tell you about it! For the guys, send out an email now about buying matching ties. Then go ahead and buy the matching ties yourself because they aren't responsible enough for this bare-minimum task.

☐ **SEND SAVE THE DATES**—Yes, you need to send Save the Dates *and* invitations. If you don't send a Save the Date, how will your guests know that they're going to be getting an invitation somewhere down the line? A Save the Date is like an invitation to get an invitation and is very important. It is in no way a waste of paper or an objectively dumb thing.

☐ **ORDER CAKE**—As is the case with everything in a wedding, this cake is different from a regular cake in that it is more expensive and isn't as good. It's an overpriced, tasteless, styrofoam tower that will leave you craving a fifty-cent Chipwich.

☐ **PLAN CEREMONY**—That's right, you still have to plan the whole ceremony! Even if you're just going to let a priest do his thing, you'll still have to pick out the readings and the people to read them!

If you're not doing a religious ceremony, you'll have to come up with a bunch of secular bullshit to fill it out. Like a wine ceremony, a ribbon-tying ceremony, or a bullfight.

☐ **BUY/DESIGN PROGRAMS**—A piece of paper for guests to fan themselves with during your surprisingly long, mid-ceremony bullfight.

☐ **BUY RINGS**—A wedding band is the engagement ring's boring cousin. They all look the same. Just go to a jewelry store and pick one of the inexpensive metals like Tungsten or Pure Rust.

☐ **SEND INVITATIONS**—Even though anyone you would ever want to come to your wedding has an email address, sending out electronic invites is considered tacky and you have to send out paper ones. Why? Because you have been sold the fiction of a wedding being your "special day" when in fact it is catered specifically to the old people in your family who don't know how to use computers.[21]

☐ **GET MARRIAGE LICENSE**—Ah, yes. The piece of paper that you could have just signed at the beginning and been done with it all. Further infuriating proof that a wedding is quite literally all for show.

☐ **PLAN REHEARSAL DINNER**—A rehearsal dinner is like a different wedding on the night *before* your wedding. Go back and redo everything, but replace the word "wedding" with "rehearsal dinner"!

---

21 Although you can use electronic invitations to weed out undesirables. More on that later.

A wedding is an emotional tornado—a time when dads cry, religious aunts dance to "Bitch Better Have My Money," and your friends from different circles sleep with each other. It's a powder keg of emotions, and it's on your shoulders to make sure no one lights a match. Which brings us to yet *another* list: the guest list.

The guest list isn't just about who *you* want there. It's about who your partner wants there. And your parents. And your partner's parents. And your partner's parents' parents, who, believe it or not, are still alive.

Have you ever tried to order a pizza with a group of people? Everyone's needs are so different, you end up with some half–sausage and olives, quarter-Hawaiian, quarter-vegan monstrosity that no one feels good about. That's what your guest list is going to look like. Just a hot mess of pineapples and soyzzarella.

But just because your invite list is a shit show doesn't mean your wedding has to be.

HOW TO DISCOURAGE PEOPLE YOU DON'T LIKE FROM COMING TO YOUR WEDDING

Deciding who to invite to your wedding and who to stop being friends with forever can be one of the most harrowing parts of the planning process. Don't be intimidated! Start with a short guest list. Who do you *need* at your wedding? This should include people like your immediate family, grandparents, and close friends. If you're on the fence about someone, ask yourself: Would having this person there make the day more special? If you have to ask, the answer is probably no!

Next, ask your parents who *they* need at the wedding. This will be people like your aunts, uncles, cousins, second cousins, their kids, their kids' kids, your dad's poker buddies, your mom's work friends, that couple they met on the cruise, some kid your dad remembers from your little league team, *his* dad, the UPS guy, and anyone else they've had a passing conversation with since 1972. Oh, and they all get +1s.

Now you've got six hundred people coming to your wedding and you don't know five-hundred-fifty of them. Eek! The only way to get a handle on your wayward guest list is to stand up to your parents. And since you're not going to do that, you need to find other ways to dam the river of randos flooding your wedding. That means discouraging people you don't like from attending. How do you do that?

Make It a Destination Wedding. Your *real* friends and family will travel as far as it takes to see you exchange vows. Your mom's coworker Susan, who has strong opinions about Muslims on Facebook, will not. She's there to mooch a free meal. Unfortunately for her, she's gonna have to work for her beef medallions. Ask Susan and the rest of her unwanted ilk to book a six-hour flight to the wedding and watch the herd dwindle! This is one mass extinction we can get behind.

Have It on a Sunday. A Sunday destination wedding means that all of your guests will have to use a vacation day to travel home that Monday. That's inconvenient for your guests, but convenient for you because you don't want them there anyway. If Great Uncle Larry can't get off work, Great Uncle Larry can't be there to complain about your gay friends. And that's great, because we're pro-gay and staunchly anti–Great Uncle Larry.

Only Send out Email Invites. Your young, tech-savvy peers will applaud you for "going paperless" and that old couple from your mom's church who share a Hotmail account won't see it until their son comes home for Easter. Perfect! There are two people over the age of seventy that you want at the wedding and their names are Grandma and Grandpa. Every other old person can eat a *cold ham sandwich*.[22] Make this plan foolproof by having a one-day turnaround on the RSVP! Preferably on a website that's confusing to use.

Adults Only. People love their kids, almost as much as we love not having them at our wedding. Tell your third cousin Gretchen that her children aren't invited and third cousin Gretchen might be so insulted that she doesn't show up herself. That's fine, because you've *never even met* third cousin Gretchen. She's a goddamn stranger.

Appetizers Only. Everyone loves a free meal, but you don't want everyone at your wedding. Tell them you won't be serving dinner. "Ceremony at 3:00, followed by *light appetizers*." Your friends will be disappointed, but it will be worth it when your aunt's boyfriend RSVPs "no."

At this point, anyone who agrees to come to your wedding has passed the test. Reward them with the most bitchin' appetizer spread they've ever witnessed. We're talkin' shrimp cocktail, meat in those little cupcake-holder things, and enough cheeses to make a Papa John's Tuscan Six Cheese Pizza. If any of your unwanted guests *still* somehow makes it through the filter, use the seating chart on the right to go your whole wedding without seeing them!

---

22 Dick.

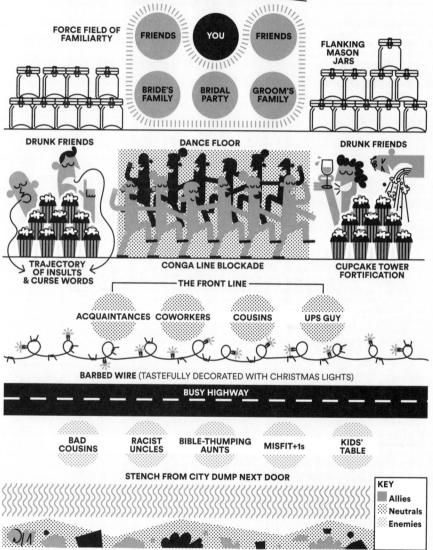

Honestly, it's kind of a blessing in disguise that you can't invite everyone you want. You are going to be doing things at your wedding that should only be seen by your closest, most forgiving, nondisclosure-agreement-signing friends. That's because, in addition to the guest list, you will also have to compromise on your itinerary. Old people love their stupid traditions. And what is a wedding but honoring old people's stupid traditions?

You may be tempted to skip the garter toss, since watching a bunch of single dudes compete to touch a woman's inner thigh is downright sad. Tough nuts, cuz for some reason, your grandma wants to see this go down. Start stretching, because you are gonna be tossing a lot of outdated things, including any notion that you are cool or progressive.

A LIST OF OUTDATED TRADITIONS YOU WILL BE FORCED TO PARTICIPATE IN

- The bouquet toss
- The garter toss
- The father/daughter dance
- The push-up contest between the groom and the father of the bride
- The chasing and hog-tying of the bridesmaids by the groomsmen
- The removal of the bride's NuvaRing in the middle of the dance floor
- The singing of the American National Anthem
- The mother/son dance
- The mother of the bride and the mother of the groom take the bride aside and teach her how to give a blow job
- The flower girl toss

- The medieval march of shame of every unmarried woman
- The eating of the bridal bouquet
- The bride sits on the lap of the groom's favorite uncle
- The groomsmen rate the attractiveness of the women on the bride's side on a scale of 1–10
- The bride apologizes to the father of the groom for each of her past sexual partners
- The best man tells a detailed story of the groom losing his virginity
- The Electric Slide
- The men in attendance all measure their penises and anyone bigger than the groom is politely asked to leave
- The groomsmen chop down a tree while chanting, "Men!"
- The bridesmaids quietly tiptoe through the dance floor, whispering "women" to anyone who notices them
- The maid of honor gives a speech and then chooses a husband, right then and there
- The groom attempts to bench-press the bride and if he can't, the marriage documents are burned
- The Cupid Shuffle

Phew, that's a lot of outdated, sexist traditions! On to more modern, sexist traditions!

CHOOSING YOUR SIGNATURE SEXIST WEDDING COCKTAIL

Having a signature wedding cocktail is as obligatory as the wedding itself! Really lean into gender stereotypes here. The groom's cocktail should be aggressively manly, so that the guests can picture his big, meaty schlong, and the bride's should be aggressively feminine as proof that she will do his dishes.

For the guy, start with whiskey. Because if there's one thing men and the women trying desperately to impress them like, it's whiskey.

JAKE'S WOOD-CHOPPING COCKTAIL THAT HE ONLY DRINKS WHEN THE BEER RUNS OUT

INGREDIENTS

· whiskey
· very bitter bitters
· muddled Playboy articles (not the girls, just the journalism everyone keeps trying to make a thing)

PRESENTATION

— Combine ingredients. Garnish with whipped shaving cream and a wood chip rim.

— Serve to some girl who won't shut up about how "I have, like, only guy friends. I just get along better with guys!"

For the lady, just throw a bunch of juice into some other juice-like stuff to make a pink thing. Because she's a girl!

CANDACE'S PINK BEYONCÉ TAMPON
_____

INGREDIENTS

· cranberry juice
· grenadine
· strawberry sherbet
· glitter
· the goo of two whole glow sticks

PRESENTATION

—   Combine ingredients. Serve frozen in a diva cup.

NOTE: You might notice there's no alcohol. It's fine. No one who is drinking it wants alcohol, they just want a dessert that they can blame dancing slutty on.

With the most important part of wedding planning out of the way—choosing a Beyoncé-themed cocktail—the big day is right around the corner. The day that every piece of pop culture has convinced you will be the best day of your life. But guess what?

With all the bridal magazines, reality shows, and Hollywood end-ings, there are a lot of expectations surrounding your big day. You've got people telling you that your wedding will be the best day of your life. And that may be true for some. But it's important to remember that those people are fucking losers.

Allow us to explain.

The average age to get married is twenty-eight. Most people who say that their wedding was the best day of their life peaked at twenty-eight. They went to high school, maybe college, then met someone, got engaged, had the *best day of their entire life* inside a barn covered in Christmas lights, and then proceeded to live for another sixty meaning-less years. At least the high school quarterback who peaked at sixteen had a modicum of talent. Most people *don't* make the varsity team. Most people *do* get married at some point. It's a non-accomplishment. It's like winning a coin flip. "Congratulations, you got heads! Here, I bought you the oven mitt from your registry."

Imagine, after millions of years of human evolution, that your great-est day on Earth is kicked off with two hours in church with a flower pinned to your shirt. If you're going to peak at twenty-eight, *at least* do it on the honeymoon—with a margarita in your hand, sunbathing, after your third tantric sex session of the day.

OK, we're being cynical. But it's not just snarky li'l bastards like us who think wedding pageantry is overblown. Statistically, the more you spend on a wedding, the more likely you are to get divorced. (Google it if you don't believe us, this shit comes straight from the *PBS NewsHour*—and they made *Sesame Street*.) That's probably because some couples are more concerned with having crystal champagne flutes for the toasts than the long-term emotional, *legal* commitment they are about to make. The best day of their marriage was the first one: now they're at an Olive Garden, buttering bread, praying that the waiter comes back to break the quiet tension that has become their everyday Hell.

Have we bummed you out on weddings? Good! We've undone some of the brainwashing of the commercial wedding industry and lowered your expectations. Your wedding day will not be perfect. You will forget to eat. Your cousin Lenny won't show up, even though he RSVP'd and you paid for his plate, that dick. Your stupid ass wedding planner will forget to put wine in the wine cups for the wine ceremony even though it's right there in the fucking program, Karen. But there will also be lots of good things! You'll have all your friends in one room. Your family will say nice things to each other. You will take great joy in not tipping Karen because a tip is for exemplary service and she sucks.

It will be a really good day, but it won't be some out-of-body experience as advertised. You'll be the same couple you always were, standing in front of an officiant, who's standing in front of a PA system, causing some serious mic feedback. And when it's all over, there won't be a sudden transformation: you'll just look at each other and say, "Whoa, weird! I guess we're married!"

And that's pretty fucking cool!

After the wedding, it's time to head to the honeymoon suite for the *main event*—going to sleep.

Look, a lot of great sex awaits. You've got a honeymoon full of celebratory consummation. You're gonna be gettin' nasty in the glow of the Caribbean sunset/Eiffel Tower/midday sun bouncing off Theodore Roosevelt's shiny-ass forehead at Mount Rushmore. Not to mention all the sex instigators that lie in your future: the promotions at work, the anniversaries, the birthdays, the relief after returning home from ten sexless days visiting your parents. See? So much good boneage awaits you!

Except on your wedding night.

You will be two very tired, quasi-drunk people who just want to go to sleep. Not "I danced too much" tired, but "my bones ache" and "my brain feels like it was pulled out through my nose like they do when they preserve mummies" tired. You will have spent the last forty-eight hours with a fake smile plastered across your face. Even when it was a real smile, you will have seen the photographer in the corner of your eye and thought, "Shit, I need to turn this smile up to 11 or this candid moment isn't gonna be worth the 9 × 12 frame I got for it."

By the time you finally retreat to your honeymoon suite, chambers, cabana, silo, igloo, broom closet, or whatever special lodging the venue threw in for free,[23] it will be as a married couple. And it's expected that you'll consummate the marriage. You *could* just wait to have sex until you actually feel like it, but you'd have to do that with the knowledge that even the staunchly religious get nasty on their wedding night.

---

23 Overcharged you for something else to cover the cost of.

Can your sexual ego handle the idea of being less adventurous than your mom's church friends? Ours couldn't.

So we phoned it in.

You don't have to have good sex to consummate the marriage. You just have to have sex. That's a really low bar. Follow our detailed instructions below to take and/or give one for the team!

1. *Remove just enough clothing to get the job done.*

2. *Get the job done.*

3. *Sleep.*

You did it! You had married sex. And the best part is, it can only get better!

EPILOGUE

YOU DID IT, ALL THANKS TO US!

It's over. You never have to plan a wedding again (hopefully)! No more designing Save the Date magnets or getting voicemails from caterers or deciding between photo packages or logistical emails about matching ties or visiting rustic-chic venues or meeting with ministers or ring fittings or dress fittings or bridesmaid dress fittings or tuxedo fittings or ANY FITTINGS PERIOD. EXCLAMATION POINT! All that's left to do is relax. And send out a couple hundred Thank You notes. Shit, you forgot about those, didn't you?

Oh, well. Bear down and fart 'em out so you can get on with your life. Soon, the trauma of wedding planning will be behind you. That is, until you receive a bridal magazine in the mail and drop to your knees, clawing at your face as the memories come rushing back. Once you're on their mailing list, you're on it 'til the day your kids bury you (under a pile of bridal magazines, of course). Brace yourself for the upcoming flood of baby coupons. Brands are so good at predicting your biological clock!

When the fairy dust of the wedding has settled, you'll be left alone, together. The relationship will experience a severe downtick in hubbub. And that's a good thing. No more arguments about cummerbunds. You can get back to doing the things you love—like not talking about cummerbunds. Plus, if either of you suffered a mental breakdown because of the wedding, you now have visitation rights at the hospital!

You've probably asked your married friends if it feels different to be married. In our opinion, it does. And since our opinion is *correct*, we can 100 percent guarantee that it will change your relationship. Whether that's for the better or for the worse depends entirely on what remains when the excitement has waned: the *partnership* that out-lasts the spotlight, the streamers, the speeches, and the seven-tiered cupcake tower.

Partnership is the key word here. Love is nice, but it gets mixed up in lust, limerence, and all kinds of other fleeting words that begin with *L*. Real love isn't about getting butterflies in your stomach or making big, sweeping romantic gestures. It's nice to take bubble baths together or do whatever it is romantic people do, but that's not day-to-day love. That's not a *partnership*.

A partnership is walking to the drugstore at 2 A.M. to get antacid because she stuffed her face with Indian food even though she knows chutney wreaks havoc on her insides. A partnership is still saying, "I love you," as you head out the door in the morning even though he's been kind of a grumpy bastard since he woke up. A partnership is getting down on your hands and knees and cleaning up your cat's shit together because he got some on his tail and then whirled it around the room like a fucking idiot. No person should have to face a whirling-shit-tail alone.

Real love is about taking responsibility for each other. And responsibility is good, despite what punk bands and Garfield comics might tell you. Find someone who puts in the effort and you'll grow together instead of growing apart. That's someone you can depend on. Some-body who isn't scared off by complications—who doesn't leave the threat of a breakup looming. Good partnerships are adult, but in a fun way. Like "stay out all night on a Tuesday cuz no one can tell us not to" fun.

Your joy will be multiplied because you'll have someone to share it with, and your sorrow will be halved because you'll have someone to bitch about your sorrow to. Life's a boxing match, baby, and you're in each other's corners, fixing up cuts, offering a little advice, then sending each other back out there to FUCK. SHIT. UP. You can even team up on your problems, which would be illegal in a boxing match, but is totally great in real life!

When you think about the future, you'll think about how it applies to "we" instead of "I." You will be a team. You'll take great comfort in knowing that you've got a best friend to bring, or follow, along to everything. It's like when you were starting high school and found out that one of your buddies was assigned to the same class and it just made everything a little easier. Like that, but all the time, and applied to everything.

You get help with decisions. You get the satisfaction of knowing you helped with *their* decisions. You'll work toward common financial goals while makin' that shared *BANK!* You'll learn to comfort and please someone in and out of the bedroom (hey-o). You'll even develop a weird, psychic language with each other, like twins do. But, like, Doublemint twins. Not *The Shining* twins.

Stability. Dependability. The toughness to weather any storm. These are words that describe great relationships and also, really good car tires.

Congratulations to you. But also, to us. For throwing you over our shoulder and carrying your deadweight down the aisle. You took a few steps out of the gate when you bought the book, then we took the baton and ran with it. But we couldn't have done it without you—the warm body who listened to our advice. We wish you a happy, healthy life together.

And for you to rate this book five stars across all platforms. Like, honestly? You kind of owe us.

ACKNOWLEDGMENTS

This book wouldn't have been possible without a lot of great people and a delightful chain of events. Thank you to our manager, Joel Zadak, for giving us the idea to write this book in the first place and pitching the title *Live Together, Work Together, Sleep Together*, which we still might use for our memoirs. Thanks to our literary agents, Todd Shuster and Elias Altman, for guiding us newbies through the early process and introducing us to the smart, cool, attractive people at Abrams.

A big thank you to our editor, David Cashion, for helping us translate our humor to literary form for the first time—and an even bigger thank you to David for not killing us when we asked for an extension while working on the TV show. Thanks to our illustrator, John Devolle, for working off our crappy little sketches and turning them into works of art that are way cooler than the source material deserves. And thanks also to Gabriel Levinson and Devin Grosz at Abrams for their help.

Thank you to our friend and talented writer Katherine DiSavino for giving us quick feedback and invaluable notes when our deadlines were fast approaching. Thanks to Sam Reich and our friends at CollegeHumor for giving us our first opportunities as comedy writers.

Finally, thank you to our families for their continued support—although we hope you didn't actually read the book because we said fuck like fifty times.

ABOUT THE AUTHORS

Emily Axford and Brian Murphy are the creators and stars of the show *Hot Date* for the cable network Pop. They both appear on TruTV's *Adam Ruins Everything* and were staff writers for CollegeHumor. Their videos have over 250 million views across YouTube and Facebook, so you've probably seen them make out in your feed.

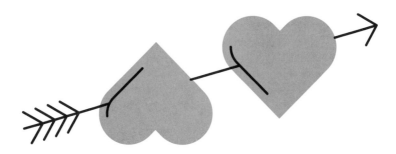